Summoned by a Stroke

An Homage to Love,
Relationship, and Living Life Fully

SUMMONED BY A STROKE

*An Homage to Love,
Relationship, and Living Life Fully*

JUDY FRIESEM

Copyright © 2020 by Judy Friesem
All rights reserved.

This book, or parts thereof, may not be reproduced in any form
without prior written permission of the publisher.
Published by Judy Friesem.

Front and back cover photos by Judy Friesem.

Cover and interior book design by Linn DeNesti (linndenesti.com)
with publication direction from Mi Ae Lipe (whatnowdesign.com).

Photo credits:
Pages xvi ("Ever playful"), 72, 95, 131, and 134: Greg MacDonald
Page 73: © Mark Gsellman
All other photos are used by permission.

Printed in the United States of America.

To contact the author or order additional copies:
SummonedByStroke.com

First Edition, 2020
ISBN: 978-0-578-62683-3
Library of Congress Control Number: 2019921071

Praise for *Summoned by a Stroke: An Homage to Love, Relationship, and Living Life Fully*

"Judy writes of how she and her husband Kim learned to live in what Kim described as 'sacred time,' following a stroke that shattered their previous lives. Judy's writing gives us the chance to experience with them the profoundly difficult and delightful as well as the sorrow-filled and creatively inspired discoveries they navigated along the way. This is a book to be read slowly, to savor the miracle of being summoned to live life completely in the present as it is, not as we wish it to be.

Together, and within a loving community of friends and family, Judy and Kim show us how to face obstacles as well as gifts of grace with a similar equanimity; and how to do as Itzhak Perlman did when he found how much music he could still make playing with a broken violin string. As a couple who renewed their vows to love even more deeply than before the stroke, Kim and Judy's heartfelt gratitude for life, their humor and humble courage, and especially their abiding love shine through on every page of this book."

— **Susan S. Scott, PhD**
mental health counselor and author of Healing with Nature

"What a privilege to read Judy Friesem's beautiful, tender, and breathtakingly honest reflections on her husband's stroke and all that unfolded when their lives were upended on one fine September day. Much more than a medical memoir detailing the uncertain twists and turns of life after a stroke, this book is a story of love and profound commitment, of the individual but connected journeys of lovers coming to terms with an altogether different future than one they had ever imagined. It is a story of the salvation and healing offered by friends, community, and family; by nature's prodigious and proximate wonders; and by the power of music to calm and connect. In short, this book is both a gift and a gem—a tribute to the human spirit and its capacity for resilience—it will enrich the lives of all who read it!"

— **Marcy Jackson**
cofounder and Senior Fellow of the Center for Courage and Renewal

"As the neurologist who cared for Kim during and after his hospitalization for a severe stroke, I came to know Kim from his journey as a stroke victim to a stroke survivor. From the beginning, it was clear that Kim would find a new path toward living his life with more than just adjustment to his new disability. His extensive experiences, loving relationships, and strong character that existed prior to his stroke allowed Kim to forge a new life with the help of his loving wife, Judy. I always enjoyed our visits and hearing how Kim and Judy were making new connections and developing new relationships with those who cared for him. In the end, Kim's story and this book are a testament to the fact that while a stroke can take away so many of one's abilities and one's previous life, many things are out of the reach of this injury. It is these things that not only persevere but develop in ways that are hard to fathom."

— **Sandeep Khot, MD, MPH**
neurologist at the Stroke Clinic at Harborview Medical Center and associate professor in the Department of Neurology at UW Medicine

"This is a love story—deeply felt and shared…Judy beautifully expresses how, out of the hollow spaces of grief, life emerges anew and how we never stop learning and growing. For anyone who wonders what it takes to find joy in each day, no matter how difficult, Judy and Kim's story will inspire you."

— **Marilyn Price-Mitchell, PhD**
developmental psychologist and author of Tomorrow's Change Makers

"*Summoned by a Stroke* gently walks the reader through a heartfelt story of companionship, respect, and love, written with a quiet strength and spirit in the wake of a life-altering stroke that changed everything. Judy's unwavering devotion shines through as the book guides you to unexpected light and joy."

— **Denise Callaghan**
Community Relations, Stafford Suites in Port Orchard-Assisted Living

"Judy and Kim are the gold standard of love and commitment, beautiful to experience and never forced out of a sense of obligation. It was apparent that there was no place they would rather be than in that moment with each other. In my time with Kim, he commonly had an extreme headache and was minimally mobile and fatigued. Yet he was always keenly interested in those around him; people of all ages and persuasions were drawn to his smile, bright eyes, and quick wit. A stranger was just someone he hadn't met yet. At the end of a long day of hard work in patient care, having the honor to work with someone as courageous as Kim is what makes being a physical therapist so fulfilling."

— Keith Heinzelman, DPT, MTC, CHT
physical therapist, Bainbridge Island Physical Therapy

"For fifty years, Kim felt like my closest friend in spite of the many geographical miles that separated us. While I was living a more conventional life, Kim was always on an idealistic adventure, starting with his service in Africa with the American Friends Service Committee, his resistance to the Vietnam War, his role as a teacher and a volunteer in many troubled places in the world, and a loving father and husband. Adjectives fall short in describing this wonderful, imaginative, thoughtful, quirky, humorous, idealistic, sometimes troubled, loving man. I like to think most of his quiet humor.

Judy's beautiful descriptions of her relationship with Kim are quite extraordinary and very moving to me as his long-time friend. In writing this, I feel she was able to relive so many meaningful times and with such a range of emotion."

— Andy Griffiths
*Brown University friend of Kim's
and past Administrative Dean, College of the Atlantic*

These "letters from the edge" are an intimate glimpse
into the lives of husband and wife
Kim Bush and Judy Friesem, two people
learning to cope with and thrive
after the devastating effects of a debilitating stroke.

Deeply honest, thought-provoking, and inspiring,
this open-hearted account reveals much.
It is a poignant homage to love,
relationship, and living life fully.

It will inspire.

*I dedicate this book to Kim's beautiful and strong daughter,
Megan Bush, who graced her father's last years
with love and the gift of two extraordinary grandsons.*

*And I write in honor of the light within each of us that glows
ever brighter when forged in the heat and pressure
of life's inevitable challenges.*

CYNIC

by Kim Bush

You stand
one-legged alone
on the edges of many
estuaries,

a glum, brooding silhouette.

Impatient with flighty pleasures
of godwits and gulls
you scowl and scold,
and, with a single raspy complaint,
push off

in search of another solitary edge.

Table of Contents

Foreword xiii

Prologue: The Man 1

Part 1: An Unexpected Journey 6

Part 2: Simple Pleasures 17

Part 3: Moments of Connection 25

Part 4: Radical Acceptance 34

Part 5: Music Heals 55

Part 6: Ever a Teacher 70

Part 7: The Comfort of Rituals 84

Part 8: Grief and Praise 99

Part 9: Sacred Time 112

Part 10: Letting Go 123

Epilogue 128

Kimberly Bush, Jr.—Obituary 129

Acknowledgments 132

Reading Group Questions 135

Foreword

I have known Judy and Kim for many years. Kim was a meditation student and early member of our Seattle Insight Meditation board of directors. He and I taught a tailor-made class for teens interested in meditation. It was obvious that he was in his element, completely comfortable and relaxed with this age group, and I was awkwardly following his lead. We stayed connected in friendship through all the intervening years. I was also privileged to be one of several friends who formed a graduate advisory committee for Judy's master's program at Antioch College. Years later I officiated Kim and Judy's marriage in our backyard. In 2007, Kim suffered a massive stroke that left him partially disabled until his death in 2011. As the title of this book suggests, this is the telling of a love story narrated around the most challenging set of circumstances imaginable.

Summoned by a Stroke is an alive and uplifting account of a deep and abiding affection that outward circumstances could not touch. Judy's straightforward, honest style lays out the challenges she and her husband faced without sentimentality or resentment. This is a book of strength and fortitude, courage and trust. Grace fills these pages as we are ushered through episode after episode of situations that would have decimated anyone of lesser wisdom. As Judy states, "We're living out the lives we've been given, best we can…We're happy together, perhaps more than ever. We're a strong team long as we focus on what we can do, not on what we can do no longer." Later in the book, she writes, "Peace in our hearts. We're happy and remain utterly grateful. How fortunate we are to be surrounded by so much care and to feel so meaningfully engaged in life!"

To say this book is inspiring is insufficient praise, for it is much deeper and life-validating in its breadth than any single word can encompass. It raises the bar of our own potential as we face our inevitable difficulties. In effect, this book says, This is what is possible, and then challenges us in our own responses. It shocks us out of complacency because through Judy and Kim's example, we all feel what is humanly possible.

As a meditation teacher, the wisdom I attempt to impart can be partially summarized by this precept: If we want to be happy, simply live with things as they are, not as we wish them to be. In all honesty, I am imperfect in my ability to live this principle even after fifty years of practice. I remember my wife and I visiting Judy and Kim a few times after his stroke and the two of us walking away astounded by the integration of this wisdom into Kim and Judy's lives. They seemed to have no forward worry or backward despair. Kim and Judy did not seem to linger on what could have been or what might be. They were simple living the moment as it was without regret or remorse. Judy calls it "adapting and accepting." I call it a sacred life well lived.

As I read through this manuscript, I am further struck by the practicality of their actions throughout this period. Judy and Kim did not seem hesitant to ask for help when needed, allowing other people's love to flow in and renew their own. They speak about the day-to-day living of both caregiving and care receiving, and that true love needs both outward action and inward replenishment. This book gives equal measure and gratitude to their community that met their struggles with concrete support and effort. Their interdependence upon others spread their love throughout the collective, and everyone was nourished.

This book avoids all stoicism or pretentiousness. On every page, Judy and Kim's humanness is laid bare. Seizures, endless therapy treatments and rehab centers, trips to hospital emergency rooms, pain and weariness, emotional highs and lows, leg cramps and spasms, difficulty swallowing, endless doctor appointments, five hours a day getting Kim in and out of bed—all happening simultaneously to the never-ending daily challenges we all face in meal preparation and daily laundry. Somehow Judy manages all of this without obvious discouragement and infuses humor, joy, wit, poetry, and beautiful prose all along the way.

The themes of trust, space, and silence are strongly emphasized throughout these pages. Surprisingly, Judy and Kim seem to discover a deeper level of inward stability as they lose more outward control, and what arises is a basic trust that many of us miss because of our undiminished abilities. Some of us count on our health, mental acuity, and fitness for our confidence and salvation, but inevitably that will come to an end, and what is left to support our meaning, purpose, and intention without these? Judy and Kim trusted silence, which is not the mere absence of sound but a unifying element that interconnects the threads of life. They knew the value of silence and used it to nourish their stamina and deepen their connection.

In Judy's words, "I've been feeling like I'm a sailboat at sea. Not lost, as I'm not far from land and can see where I want to go. Yet I cannot quite seem to get there. Tossed wildly by the winds that come out of all directions, unpredictable and harsh. I start to tack but soon as I set sail, I get sideswept by yet another gust. Nor can I set anchor, for it's too deep here. Best I can figure is to hunker down and wait, taking deep breaths, trusting that the winds too will calm, the sky will clear, and the way will open."

What does life look like when the only action we can take is to surrender, when the daily obstacles often seem insurmountable, and when we are left with only the resolve of our caring hearts? It looks like this book. Most of us are not comfortable with the word "surrender." We think it means losing our position and handing over our power and place in life, but Judy shows it to be just the opposite—an activity of strength and trust. In Judy's words, "I continue to have hope, lots of it—I just keep practicing living ever more lightly."

Was Kim's stroke a blessing, a tragedy, or both intertwined? Would the depth of this wisdom and the refined attunement of this couple's hearts have been reached without the pain of this process? Should we, as readers of this book, continually attempt to escape any hint of unpleasantness, or is there redemption within our struggles? This book encourages us to decide if a life of difficulties has any ultimate merit and how we might respond when our own inevitable struggles do arise.

I loved reading about Judy and Kim's rituals: their play, music making, "greeting the day," and stops at the "kissing station." We can learn so much about how to be content when it is our time to be "summoned by stroke" through these simple ceremonies. Rituals teach us gratitude, humility, patience, perseverance, constraint, and generosity. These playtimes speak volumes about love and love's relationship to letting go.

Our lives can be used to end our arguments with the moment so love can flourish. We sense that an unselfish love cannot fail since it redefines success by excluding failure. Quoting Judy, "I recently came across the simple reminder that in the end, what matters most is how well we lived, how well we loved, and how well we learned to let go. Maybe this is our time to practice."

Thank you, Judy and Kim. You have given us a lasting gift.

Rodney Smith
May 2019
Seattle, Washington

Kim as a baby.

Kim as a toddler.

Big brother to sister Susie.

High school yearbook photo.

Curious about the world.

Kim with attitude.

Ever playful.

Prologue
The Man

Kim stood at six foot three. He was strong, not heavy. His walk had a slight, characteristic gait to it. He walked with purpose, stood tall. There was always a slight smile on his face; his presence was welcoming. His hands were solid: they created big, useful things from wood and stone. His body loved to move; he hiked, biked, and rowed…hard.

And his eyes! His eyes were the color of the dark aquamarine of tropical waters; they saw things, he noticed. His face radiated openness and kindness. Kim was used to people being drawn to him, kids and youth especially. Women, too.

This man was playful. People would smile before greeting, in readiness for the banter. I loved to listen to him on the phone with friends, imagining the responses on the other end to his bait for laughter. He was a devoted friend, a loving and vibrant man.

There was the dark side, too. When I first met him, he was fifty-four and dissatisfied with his life. He wasn't a "good enough" teacher, hadn't accomplished what he felt was worthy of his Ivy League education. He was neither a steady father for his young daughter nor a good husband to his first wife. He had wolves eating at his heart.

We were the perfect match. I had my own demons to battle. He wouldn't let me get away with my unhealthy patterns; I held him to his integrity and demanded honesty. Both of us were strong and demanding, passionate about what we felt and believed. The hardest thing we had to do to make this relationship work was exactly what we both needed to give in order to grow.

And were we motivated! Our intensity was fueled by our spellbinding attraction to each other. I couldn't stay mad at him. He had a disarming way of cocking his head and listening hard. Never defensive, truly. When I went on with an "And another thing…" rant, spewing forth all that was unacceptable to me, he seemed to get happier. He'd cheerily say, "Really! Tell me more." It seemed that my unwillingness to bend to his will, delighted him. We found ways to wrestle with our differences and find new, creative ways through. Our respect ran deep, forged in the heat and pressure of how we lived our lives.

I met Kim later in life. He had already lived through a marriage. He had a beautiful and strong grown daughter of whom he was very proud. He had lived in many countries and spoke five languages fluently. His work ranged from being a carpenter to a high school educator to an education officer for refugees with the United Nations.

Kim was brilliant. A pile of books always stood by his bed. Astonishingly, he remembered what he read. Kim was my "Siri"; I could ask him anything. He seemed to know the most esoteric information and would hand it to me without judgment. For a chapter of his life, he was known as "Books." Learning was as important to him as food (and he sure loved his food). His curiosity about the world was insatiable. This made him a wonderful conversationalist and a deep listener. Kim was a global citizen who inspired many young people to travel and learn about other peoples, as well as themselves.

Born in 1940 to well-educated and engaged parents, Kim grew up in Connecticut on the Atlantic Ocean, where he learned to love the sea. He studied at Brown University in Rhode Island, received an MA in African history from Syracuse University in New York, and came away with a near-doctorate in African studies from the University of California.

Father Kim Sr., mother Eileen, sister Susie, and Kim.

He helped build wells for Tanzanians through the American Friends Service Committee, worked in New York City housing projects, and was arrested for anti-apartheid activities in the 1960s. He taught Swahili to Peace Corps members.

Kim met up with Louisa in Tanzania forty years after working alongside her.

In the 1970s, Kim worked as a house carpenter and also built his beloved peapod rowboat, the *Eileen R*, named after his mother. In the 1980s, he taught high school in Midland, California, then international baccalaureate history in Ecuador. From 1989 to 1992, he lived in Thailand and worked for the United Nations, establishing education and training for refugees. Kim then returned to Washington State in the mid-1990s and taught high school in Everett—always the humanities—where he covered world history, Spanish, and English literature. Kim wrote articles, book reviews, and curricula. And in 1996 I ran into him.

I first saw Kim across a crowded room at a friend's Labor Day party. I caught his eye and felt electricity charge through me. But politeness won out and I sought to greet my friend first. For the rest of the evening, I searched for him. He was not there (it wasn't a big house). Perplexed, I left disappointed and beguiled.

A photo-booth capture of when we met in 1996.

It was only weeks later that I met Kim on a blind dinner date set up by my friend, the host. He said he wasn't at the party, had never seen me. Our four-hour-plus dinner date turned things for us both and we were inseparable after that. It was only years later that he acknowledged that he had fled when he laid eyes on me at the party, intuitively sensing that his life was about to change.

But Kim was restless. He told me right away that I couldn't hold him down, that he had to travel. Within the first year of our relationship, he was off on a three-month Buddhist meditation silent retreat. I could write to him, but he couldn't answer—hardly satisfying for me who needed affirmation. And although we were both working full-time, we managed to travel to India for many months, trek in Nepal, and spend time in Cuba, all during our first few years of life together.

In 2001 we moved to Winslow Cohousing on Bainbridge Island. This proved to be providential, for living in this exceptional, community-oriented "village" not only made sense and matched our values, it also contained the weave of the support that became critical for us as we navigated the poststroke years.

We continued to travel. Kim spent eight months in the highlands of Guatemala as a human rights activist. Since we both spoke Spanish, we traveled a few times through Guatemala, went to Honduras, and then Ecuador for many weeks. In 2006 to 2007, we journeyed for seven months in eastern and South Africa, where I offered mediation training and Kim met with teachers and peace builders. Neither of us knew "vacations"; we journeyed intensely. We lived with our hosts, traveled as they did, ate alongside them, and breathed the same air; we absorbed what we could. We exchanged gifts of friendship and attention, offering what we had to share.

And so, Kim and I came home changed, having reached deeper into ourselves while growing in resiliency and connection, ever more aware of the world and our place in it. We depended on each other for strength and support. Our trust became absolute and our respect for each other was paramount. This, too, proved invaluable as our life unfolded.

In the early morning of Wednesday, September 19, 2007, I woke up disoriented from a dream I'd just had. I turned to Kim a bit shaken. I had been in free fall—nothing around me that I could recognize, no handholds, no guardrails, no ground. I had been plummeting through the darkened sky. Paradoxically, I wasn't scared, although I remember having to take deep breaths and stay calm. It was quite beautiful, actually—almost exciting.

Two mornings later it happened again, but this time I was startled. I said to Kim, "I don't like it. The Universe is preparing me for something BIG."

The following Sunday was September 23, 2007, an exquisite first day of fall. The sun was bright, the air pure. We were exuberant, grateful for the day. We decided to hike a new trail on the island. After coming up a steep path, I said something humorous that I knew Kim would respond to in play, but there was no answer. A chill moved through me; I turned. Kim had "wilted like a flower" (as he would say later) and crumpled to the ground.

Time had stopped. I instinctively knew what had happened: Kim had been struck by a severe stroke.

The stroke would leave his left side paralyzed and with compromised vision. It took his magnificent stature, his voracious love for reading, his nightingale singing voice, his independence. Yet it left him intact with—amazingly so—his tremendous capacity for humor and joy. He lived another four years. The stroke summoned Kim to be his highest self, even as it sliced through our life with the sharpest of edges. I offer you his story, our story.

This is not a guidebook, although I will describe a journey that had steep learning curves, unexpected twists and turns, plenty of breathtaking high-precipice drama, and few road signs pointing the way. We weren't prepared for the adventure; we had to take it one day at a time. The journey also brought us into full-hearted connections that may not have happened otherwise. We had remarkable opportunities to learn, so long as we honored the demands to adapt to our new life. Radical acceptance.

Nor is this a story of pity, for we lived surprisingly fully and abundantly, pulling out the marrow from a life filled with love. It's a story of generosity and abundance, of impossible demands and painful realizations, and of increasing faith and trust in a world where every moment counts.

Hiking along the California coast, a favorite playground for Kim.

Part 1
An Unexpected Journey

What follows is the blog that I kept during the four-plus years of caring for Kim after his debilitating stroke on September 23, 2007. Or, more accurately, when we were caring for each other, for he watched out for me as well.

Kim coined the word "care receiver," recognizing what it took to be the recipient of care when all he had known was extreme independence.

Kim didn't know what I wrote. The blog was my way of responding to the inquiries of his many friends and followers. And it soon became my way of staying afloat, for I needed the witnesses and the outpouring of love and attention.

I have kept the blog pretty much intact with context added where helpful. I've included many photos, some of Kim's poetry, comments from friends, and sidebars of info that I feel paint the picture of his remarkable life.

This blog starts a few weeks into Kim's recovery as I wrote late at night from Harborview, the best trauma hospital in the Pacific Northwest.

October 4, 2007

Hello Friends,

Kim is sleeping hard, hopefully recouping energy and healing. When he was awake today, we are sure we heard him speak! "Yes"—the best possible first word… and "water." I look forward to waking up tomorrow and hearing more, perhaps.

His vital signs (I wrote "sighs") are still strong. We will be moved to the floor tomorrow if a bed is available. In the meantime, I rest, assured that he is in good hands. These nurses are terrific.

I have been awed at the response today from my email. Thank you all for your care, your offers, your support.

Mustering grace, ~ Judy

October 5, 2007

Thursday was a reminder that this is a long, slow road. Deep breaths, and patience.

Kim wasn't responding as he had even a few days ago, in a place deeper than sleep. We were concerned that this was a sign of something going on in his brain, so he had another CAT scan. There was no change; vital signs are holding steady. These dips ARE the recovery.

Eleanor, a teacher at West Sound, wrote to Kim: "I think of you out rowing in your boat and long for you to come back to shore." That's it—he's working so hard to find his way through the fog and come home. That image holds me.

I do believe that he hears everything and recognizes what's familiar. It's a semi-conscious state. This healing has its own time and rhythm.

There's a good chance that Kim will be transferred to a rehab place on Bainbridge by this time next week to continue getting stronger, before beginning inpatient rehab here at Harborview.

His daughter Megan (NYC) and sister Susie (MA) are here through the weekend. Our niece Katie and husband Doug arrive on Friday from CA. If you'd like to stop by, please let me know.

Thank you all, ~ Judy

A familiar scene: Kim rowing his beloved peapod.

A Single Pull of the Oar

~ For Kim Bush ~

by Eleanor Johnson

There you go, setting off in your beloved peapod,
the boat you made yourself
out of rugged north woods of Maine
hard proven in northwest passages,
the craft you paddled to the tips of continents
and on toward the ends of nations
In one pocket you hold a gentle paradox
In the other, pieces of wisdom you turn
over and over like worry stones,
In your hold you carry things to give awa
In a wink I see that this is a test,
not a test of endurance,
you will endure
but a lark to say,
we're with you
rowing against the wind and tide
out there, beyond the point,
and not merely waving from the headlands,
craning our ears for your cheery whistle
(a thin, airy whistle now)
Today a day
like any other...

October 6, 2007

Hi Friends,

It's looking more certain that Kim will be moved to Island Health and Rehabilitation Center next week. It's close by, only a somersault away from our home in Winslow Cohousing—a gift in itself. The place is quite lovely and quiet and seems to have good rehab services, including a dog on staff! Once he regains strength, Kim will return to Harborview for their excellent inpatient intensive rehab before coming home. We're talking weeks at best, perhaps months. Such is the vision; let's hold it all lightly.

Kim was a bit more responsive today. He clearly said hello to his daughter Megan and seemed somewhat alert in the morning. We are guessing that he's taking in the poetry we're reading (in Spanish too), the songs we're singing, and the stories we're telling him about you who've called and written. I swear I saw a smile begin. Again, it'll be like this for a while, I'd guess; we know that healing is a slow and crooked road.

Sharing a poem by Rashani, which Sharon passed on to me:

> *There is a brokenness*
> *out of which comes the unbroken,*
> *a shatteredness out of which blooms*
> *the unshatterable.*
> *There is a sorrow*
> *beyond all grief which leads to joy;*
> *and a fragility*
> *out of whose depths emerges strength.*
> *There is a hollow space*
> *too vast for words*
> *through which we pass with each loss,*
> *out of whose darkness*
> *we are sanctioned into being.*
> *There is a cry deeper than all sound*
> *whose serrated edges cut the heart*
> *as we break open to the place inside*
> *which is unbreakable and whole,*
> *while learning to sing.*

In peace, - Judy

October 7, 2007

It's truly as they say—up and down, in and out of awareness. It's a hard sea to ride as hope wants to hang on to the crests. Lessons, huh.

Yesterday Kim was following a conversation between daughter Megan and his nurse El from Thailand, and clearly said "chokdi"—"good luck" in Thai. When niece Katie was explaining that she's a teacher, Kim threw in "science." Doug walked into the room and Kim reached out a hand and thanked him for the CD Doug and Katie sent three months ago! He was taking in everything and making connections that amazed us. VERY, very exciting.

Today Kim was far out to sea, almost unreachable. He managed to say "Hi" to our young friend Meskie and goodbye to sister Susie, who is returning to Massachusetts. And he did fall asleep to my singing lullabies, which delighted me. I do believe that music will be key to his healing. His head has been pounding; he handles the pain without complaining, always. Another CAT scan and questions answered to reassure us that this is to be expected—yet it's hard to witness.

Also today, Kim was unhooked from his "tele," the monitor for blood pressure, pulse, and respiration. He's been holding steady for long enough that it's no longer needed.

The improvement over the past week since his surgeries is obvious. (I am slowly learning to think in weeks, not days.) Kim works so hard to rest, to heal, to communicate. I honor his unbelievable strength.

I thank you so much for your cards, your messages, your support, and your prayers. The energy created by this community of friends is powerful and profound. We need it surely, and rest in gratitude.

With love, ~ Judy

October 9, 2007

Each day brings new surprises, so hang on as we navigate through them.

When awake, Kim tracks well and tries hard to communicate. Wish I were better at (1) guessing what topic he's on and (2) figuring out the words. I tell him that we'll both get better at it. Most of our communication happens when we're holding hands. Somehow, he manages to tell long stories with that expressive right hand, even when I think he's asleep. I love it as much as he seems to; it is enough, it is our source of comfort.

Kim is right now resting almost peacefully following a surgery to put in a PEG, a feeding tube in his stomach. It's important, for he's not yet awake enough to swallow and eat. The PEG ensures that he'll get the nutrition he needs. It's temporary, for sure. I cannot imagine Kim holding back from eating oysters and chips any longer than he has to!

All of that's good. The new complication is that they discovered a blood clot yesterday in his jugular, in his neck. The danger of that clot going to his lungs is great enough that they've decided to start him on heparin, a blood thinner. If you're able to follow all of this, you'll realize that that can spell trouble for more hemorrhaging in his brain. That's it—risky any way it's handled. Yes, it is serious.

So please know that he IS in good hands here, and that everyone is walking this tightrope best we can. Kim remains magnificent. I don't know how he still manages to maintain his dignity and beauty (bald looks good); I lose mine hourly. We do not yet know when we'll be able to transfer to Island Health; will keep you posted. I still hold out hope that it'll be within the week.

That's it for tonight. You continue to hold us in your hearts; you are in ours. We both can feel it.

Thank you, thank you. ~ Judy

October 11, 2007

I'm just back from the all-night cafe downstairs, getting Kim a bit of mint tea. The tea seems to bring a bit of comfort, though I can only put a teeny bit on a sponge and wet his lips with it. Yet that's enough to coax a request from him. His speech IS getting clearer; I'm pleased to be able to understand more.

Kim is recuperating well from his feeding tube surgery. His body is tired; he was unable to respond to much of anything yesterday. Even with that, he managed to thank the speech therapist who came by; gracious even now.

The docs say that there's nothing more keeping him here, that Kim's work now is to regain strength. They will transfer him either Thursday or Friday to Island Rehab on Bainbridge, as soon as they are satisfied with his blood levels. CAT scans continue to be uneventful, happily so. They seem to feel confident about the jugular clot breaking up. I am pleased for the report that Kim is holding steady as well. I long to return to the island, for I so miss touching home, the closeness of neighbors, access to autumn colors, the smell of fresh air.

Many of you are telling me that you are unable to focus on work or school, that you are struggling with Kim's situation. How could it not be so; I'm guessing that we are all walking around with heightened awareness of the fragility of our lives and the grace of just being here. I seem to need boundless space and quiet to sit with it and surrender to what is, what cannot be changed. I only feel grief when I mourn the loss of freedoms of the past. My practice now is to rest into each moment and not judge this change as either good or bad, just what is so. "In this moment we are safe. And in this one. This one too." and on. There is so much to learn; curiosity remains a steady friend.

Backpacking in the Olympic Mountains, which we did often.

    The hardest part for me is to watch Kim in pain. I remind myself that he probably won't remember much, will hopefully come out of this time with a sort of amnesia. Maybe I will too. I can only say again that this courageous man is remarkable, never complaining, no anger at what has been handed to him. He finds joy in reaching out time and again to a gentle voice or touch in spite of discomfort, finds a way to settle in to his new situation. May we all do so as well.

    So now I envision us climbing this different sort of mountain, finding the joy in the little gifts, ever strengthened by your love and our community. I know it's early in the morning, but I promise you I am not dreaming; this is our truth, and I remain grateful.

    Please stay in touch. As Kim awakes from this physically painful time, he will need your support and cheer more than ever, as will I.

In peace, ~ Judy

October 12, 2007

We're here! Landed at Island Health and Rehab this afternoon, literally across the street from Cohousing. I am breathing freer already, happy for the peace of this island, the view out Kim's window, the spread on the bed, softer lights, and a smiling roommate. Kim is resting easier and seems to know that he's a bit closer to comfort and home. Tomorrow I'll fill the bird feeder and add color to the planter box outside this weekend. These touches of life are exquisite and do me good.

I won't write much now; I just wanted you to visualize us here. We met the physical therapist today—she alone is worth being here. She was exceptional with Kim; I could not believe how she encouraged him to stretch. He sat up, found his balance (tricky with his injury), and is beginning to trust his new senses. He smiled, said a few words, and thanked each person for their help. Tremendous, truly. Tomorrow we meet the speech and occupational therapists. We're READY.

So, yay! On to this next big step. I cannot contain my excitement, although it's balanced equally by the sobering reality of how steep this climb is. None of it is easy. I imagine you know.

If you'd like to visit, please do call. Kim often perks up when friends show up, as long as you are able to accept that each day is different and that he may not have the energy for much. Too, I would welcome people willing to sit with him for an hour or two while I take care of things long ignored at home.

So there! Guess I'm not able to write a short update. It's healing for me to put into words what I witness each day and to know that you are journeying alongside.

Thank you for your courage, too, and for your love. - Judy

October 13, 2007

'Twas an exquisite fall day—warm sun and light breezes. Best of all, Kim got out in it. These therapists are worth their weight in gold. We'd been at Island Health and Rehab for barely 24 hours when the physical and occupational therapists joined forces to get Kim in a wheelchair, and I had the honor of wheeling him outside! Sun on his face and fresh air for the first time in weeks: soul food.

It was an uneven day, yet its highlight was that Kim asked David about his upcoming trip to Awassa, tracking not only the adventure but also the city in Ethiopia to which they're headed. I can't do as well with what I think is a whole brain. And when the therapists told him that their goal was to get him standing (exhausting for Kim), he responded that his goal was to stay perky.

So yes, in spite of everything Kim has been through these past three weeks, his spirit and humor are STRONG. That only half captures it. He's astounding. It's really clear to me that he is fully aware of what's going on and is pushing through the dense fog with all his formidable power to find new pathways to move in this broken body. He is keeping me going.

I am beginning to call on people to help spell me as well as to come greet Kim for short visits. Please do call my cell if you can come by and know that I may not pick up if we're in the middle of something but will call back ASAP. Thank you all for your cards (I'll hang them up tomorrow), food (keeping me nourished), prayers, understanding, and so much more.

With hope, ~ Judy

October 15, 2007

Hello All,

We're settling into our new home for now, enjoying the relative quiet of Island Rehab and the beauty out the window. At least I am, for Kim is still not comfortable opening his eyes for long; I think the light is hard on him. First bird at the feeder seen today, hoping she'll spread the word. Friends Marci and Chuck have added some color and cheer in the planter box. I've put up some photos of Kim in action, inspiring me to remember the strength in his now-weak body and hopefully reminding caregivers that he is much more than this tired physical presence. And the patchwork of cards you've sent is a constant joy to look at. You are with us in many ways.

Some signs of moving forward with healing: Stitches (38!) were taken out of the inverted "question mark" incision on Kim's head (that alone is worth contemplating). Today the speech therapist gave him sherbet to test his swallow ability; Kim called it "mighty tasty" and YES, managed to get it to his stomach. That bodes well for food in the near future. I try to imagine the kind of simple joy that those few spoonfuls of cold orange ice brought to his taste buds, throat, and every part of him. What a patient man he is.

Yet days are tough. He's had a fever come and go today, and his coughing isn't letting up. A pounding headache continues; I'm guessing it's a constant companion. Today his throat seemed drier than usual and his words were fewer and harder to understand; less responsive all around. Body is stiff and no doubt aches. This is not unexpected. I hear from everyone that recovery dips from day to day, that it's more important to look at the trend week to week. I have to remember that this is a long process.

Yes, he is healing. It's only been 3 weeks since the stroke, 2 since surgery. There is much hope, for his spirit remains strong, he continues to track conversations and make connections, and he is gracious and generous throughout. He's made it this far. Too, as many of you know, the expression in his right hand is a power to behold (and be held).

I thank all of you who have come by to see us to bring us cheer, stories, creative surprises, food for me, and more. I also thank those of you who haven't yet stopped by, for we will surely need your presence in the weeks to come. We are looking at the long view; Kim will grow increasingly more responsive in time.

As to what I need, you are helping me with that. If I have not yet taken you up on your caring offer, please trust that it's all registering and I will. I thank you for your understanding and for your flexibility. There are many times when I just need the solace of quiet.

I remain in awe of the outpouring of your love and care.

With deep appreciation, ~ Judy

October 17, 2007

I just left Kim sleeping peacefully, such a relief to see. I'm beginning to get a sense of this long pathway to recovery—mostly that there is no pattern. The roller coaster continues: highs and lows in the same day, sort of like the weather I suppose. If I'm not careful, I can feel like I'm going through a fall windstorm, daily. I do need to learn to put more space between us, for our connection is so strong that I feel much what he is going through. I must step back into a witnessing role and allow Kim his journey. Such humility, patience, and deep respect is being summoned from me these days.

The humorous side is that I find myself so focused that I am ditzy when out in the other real world, moving so slowly with all antenna on "full-alert" that it's taking me longer to find words. I love that you are so generous with me. Have I been getting a boost in aging?

Kim still has an intermittent fever (that spiked to 102 today), severe pain in his head and behind his right eye, and trouble swallowing. His chest X-ray was clear—so phew, no pneumonia. Yet he does have a urinary tract infection, which I understand could be the cause of both the fever and headache. Let's hope that once the antibiotics kick in, he'll come back to life.

Although Kim's been "far away" all day with neither words nor response to people, he HAS moved mountains once again. The undaunted physical and occupational therapists got him up and out of bed and into his chair. In spite of pain, the thrill of moving on his own was enough for Kim to somehow marshal his limited energy…and he wheeled himself down the hall!! Pam and Ed were there to witness in case I doubt my memory. Watch out world, for this man has power to burn.

Rehab is tough; it takes incredible resources. I have been asked to help Kim save his energy for the hard work ahead by requesting friends to visit only midafternoon on, after his therapy is done for the day. Short and sweet, and on the quiet side. It helps me if you can call and let me know you're coming so I can limit the number of people by his bed at one time. (Can you imagine such a community of support? I think the staff is a bit awed by it as well!) You have been so understanding and flexible, making it easier for me to balance everyone's wishes, and I thank you.

I will wake with a happy heart wondering what the day will bring. ~ Judy

Taken by a curious bystander as we were leaving the beach.

Part 2
Simple Pleasures

We are in a steep learning curve. What we once took for granted is now an exception, such as swallowing. And breakfast. And home. The simplest of things is a gift. We are being tested.

October 18, 2007

Hello All,

Just a quick one tonight, to send good news.

Kim was feeling quite a bit better today though not always able to respond. Yes, he was in his chair for quite a while…and he passed the first swallow test, which means he's now allowed ice water with a spoon. He thanked the speech therapist after each swallow. His graciousness and gratitude and patience are stunning. His early morning request was for "breakfast"; I have hope he'll have his wish soon.

His gift to me today was to reach out and stroke my head, and to thank me for my loving care. Imagine.

Hope is strong. ~ Judy

October 20, 2007

I know it's been a while since I last sat down at the computer. Part of it is that I hit my limit and needed to go into silence. The other part is that we are in another curve.

Kim has been working hard to be present for therapy, yet the pain behind his eye has been so extreme that he's been unable to stay fully present. More sleep, speech more slurred. Still tracking and reaching out to people, but enough signs for concern that his doctor ordered a CAT scan yesterday afternoon to check for what might be causing the pain. Within 15 minutes we were in an ambulance being whisked to Seattle.

Back at Harborview, though hopefully this will be a short stay. His CAT scan came out clear: no new bleeding. YAY for that. They think it's the urinary tract infection that is the cause and will keep us here for another day or so to see if Kim responds to the new antibiotic. Just to rule out any brain infection, he'll have an MRI today as well.

It's good to be here right now for this level of attention. I can only say, yet again, that I continue to learn patience, acceptance, and "flow" from Kim, who shows no signs of impatience or frustration. He seems to just ride with what's happening—the willow branch in a windstorm.

I can hope that we will return to Bainbridge in another day or so, although I know better than to plan. Our room is waiting at Island Rehab. Will let you know more as we move through the days.

Thanks for asking about what you can do—you're doing it right now, staying with us and keeping us in your thoughts and heart. Thank you too for your wonderful messages, which cheer me daily.

With care, ~ Judy

October 23, 2007

I left you last on Saturday morning, having arrived back at Harborview to try to get at what's at the core of Kim's downswings. A CAT scan, chest X-ray, and MRI later, we can happily tell you that there's NOTHING visible on the brain or lung level to cause more distress. That's absolutely wonderful news.

As with so many things in life, the trouble is brewing closer to home in a much more obvious place. Besides the UTI (urinary tract infection), which we know can cause many symptoms, we've learned that Kim has also been dehydrated and hungry. Really hungry. If the scales at the hospital are to be believed, Kim has lost over 40 pounds in a month. Even if it's half that, it's alarming. So put those 3 things together: UTI, dehydration, and hunger and anyone would have a migraine, forget about also surviving a stroke and brain surgery x2. I honestly do not know how he holds it all, let alone with dignity intact.

So yes, outrageous. Things will change fast, I predict, once we get these basics rebalanced. The infection is gone (on new antibiotics now)…we hope to be done with the catheter soon…Kim's now okayed for oxycodone for pain, especially in the eves where any loopiness won't interfere with therapy…and we're back on the rehab track. Much reassured, energy renewed.

Pam and I toured Harborview's rehab unit, supposedly one of the top 3 in the country. Watery eyes as I imagined Kim strong enough to participate fully, relearning and reclaiming his body, stretching his extraordinary intelligence, creativity, and resourcefulness in new and unimagined ways.

Snippets of cherished memories from this demanding weekend at Harborview: Lummi Island friend Pam and her daughter Sarah (nurse and soon-to-be first-year resident) brought sunshine and stories into our dark corner of the room, asked critical medical questions, and bought Kim a 100% cashmere knit cap—a stroke of genius. They spelled me while I took off for some fresh air, returning with plants for Kim to touch and smell. New senses opened for me too, for I wouldn't have believed the variety of life in a 5-block inner-city radius, including lavender and rosemary and flowers in bloom!

Joe, Mimi, and Linnaea brought a guitar and voices so beautiful that I swear even Kim teared up. Soothed us all (including our loony roommate) and called in spirit from all corners of the earth.

And Jeff, Alison, and daughters Melanie and Maya stopped by last night with gifts, including homemade apple cake, a tissue ghost and mummy to keep Kim company, and the kind of humor and play that only kids can bring: "Guess what? Chicken butt!" jokes. Had to be there, for to hear Kim give the punch line and see him smile is priceless.

We're now back on Bainbridge, hallelujah. It's GREAT to be here where the sun is streaming through the window, the lilies Megan brought are in full bloom, your cards are like wildflowers perking us up, and the staff seems genuinely happy to see us back. Our room has waited. It's a place to heal as well as work, for Debra the physical therapy director has already gotten Kim up and pushing through the pain of stiffness.

I daresay we're in a new place with the ground perhaps a bit firmer. Kim really does seem a bit more lucid and ready to communicate; I predict real food in his future before long. I know better than to plan or expect or ask, yet I do feel renewed. Kim's spirit miraculously seems to remain strong; there are breaks in the dense bank of clouds.

Last week we were adjusting to life on the Island; this week I hope to figure out a pattern around Kim's therapy that will also allow me a sustainable path. Let's try 6:00–7:30 weekdays for visiting, free-er on weekends; please call me if you'd like to come by. We need your energy and cheer, whether in person, cards, or email messages. You are weaving a fantastic nest of comfort and support around us.

Deep breaths and gratitude, - Judy

Joe and his daughter Linnaea with Kim on Blake Island, Washington.

Kim being delighted by Maya and Melanie.

OCTOBER 25, 2007

Today is a historic day. Not only is Kim's headache easing visibly, he was awake and alert most of the day, engaging in short meaningful conversations, and most miraculous of all—he ATE FOOD. Not even the baby food kind but REAL mashed potatoes, fish, and steamed carrots; all recognizable. Can't say I get how it all works: tube feeding for weeks, water (just graduated to sparkling water 2 days ago) for another week, now an honest-to-goodness meal. Maya the speech therapist says it'll still be soft food for a while, but I think Kim'll be ready for Thanksgiving if not Halloween. I'm incredulous.

It's all true. Perhaps my Mother Bear rampage yesterday helped to move things along (thanks to nurse friends Pam and Cheryl for the nudging and coaching). It really might be as simple as that: increasing his fluids and food intake. Maybe it's just the "up" part of the ride, could be the full moon, no matter. Today I could talk with Kim and mostly understand his responses. I am THRILLED to have my sweetheart back and communicating.

We're not talking small talk, either. This morning he spoke of fears of the future. We are just beginning to imagine, and that's tremendous. He said that this takes trust and is "the ultimate test." No kidding. I was able to tell him of the mountain of support you are, and I think he understood some of it. Not even I can fathom it all. He nodded when I quietly said that we have love enough between us and around us to weather anything.

"Patient" be gone, "in rehab" we are. Forget the daytime hospital gowns—we're getting dressed and sitting up every day from now on. Our challenges are changing; now it's critical to manage the intense pain he has in the joints in his left knee, hip, and shoulder. Picture arthritis exacerbated by lying in bed for a month without the energy to keep his joints aligned. We also hope to make strides in eating, balancing, and strengthening, to grow comfortable in his wheelchair, and to gain weight. It's truly exciting to be here.

Yesterday marked one month since the stroke. I believe we have both come to accept what is. "Simple pleasures," he said after his first sip of sparkling water yesterday. We are beginning again to appreciate life in all of its many expressions. We wish you the same.

Love to you, ~ Judy

October 27, 2007

I just want to start by saying that you are incredible. Your words are poetry, cards and messages keep rolling in, gifts don't quit—from homemade breads and soups and gifts of color and play to responsibilities taken care of and the "KB Fund" magically growing. I hear that West Sound Academy had a cake walk tonight at their Fall Fest to help raise money for our expenses! Unbelievable. Seems we're all inspiring each other to greater heights or more profound depths perhaps. As Kellen said tonight, it's times like this that call out our greatness. I think we all are practicing. We honor you as well.

Each day has its firsts. Two days ago was Kim's first meal, yesterday his first shower, and today was the first time he fed himself and drank from a cup—harder than it may sound. He learns instantly: one try and he's got it. A new definition for Lifelong Learner. No wonder he's such an amazing teacher! I was able to give Kim his first breakfast today: hot cereal and applesauce. He quietly began to moan and I asked if he was in pain or purring. A "chorus of purrs" he said, happy for the warm food.

Kim also had his first acupuncture treatment today, a gift from the heart of Annie Allender Robbins who's been working with us for many years (she now practices in Seattle). Annie radiates health and wholeness and tender care. She could clearly feel his chi active and strong in both sides of his body and spoke of how acupuncture is part of healing for all "stroked" people in China. I'll learn more; I'm fascinated. Kim wanted to show off his ability to swallow for her; glad to see that he's got his pride intact!

And tomorrow massage therapist Alexis will come to see if her hands can help. We're drawing from all sources, working with body and psyche and spirit. Kim's looking good, even more beautiful to me if that's possible. His vitality shines through even though he's still in quite a bit of pain. I also see how, as his physical pain lessens, his awareness and psychic pain increase. This just might be one of the hardest changes one can go through in a life: abrupt, shocking, cutting deeply through every aspect of living. He said he felt discouraged and hopeless this morning; by evening he was back to smiling and even being raunchy—the old Kim undaunted. We've started working on a Halloween costume…

So that's it for now. These last few days have been close to amazing (how can it be that we were in Harborview ER just one week ago?). I'll hold it lightly for I know about roller coasters by now, yet marrying the sobering reality with a steady dose of curiosity for what next week might bring.

Blessings to us all, ~ Judy

October 29, 2007

I wasn't going to write tonight as it's been a hard weekend with Kim more tired and a bit less responsive; headache seems to have returned. I'm thinking it's just the turmoil of the brain as it remembers. Working on not worrying, and so far I'm okay.

He's had some lovely moments with Corbin (last June's graduate), moments when he's been both present and full of gratitude. Still purring about food. And today Missoula buds Archie and Cheryl arrived (yet another trip out!) to help us both. With Cheryl being a rehab nurse with a mission, Kim might just have to get better fast.

I had to pass this on before I sleep: I just went to the website that fellow West Sound Academy teacher and friend Greg McDonald has put together, and the photos he's posted of Kim are terrific. He's captured Kim in many moods—playful and alive and exquisite. Please do check out kimbush.net. And please do keep these images of Kim with you. He IS in this unusually still body, ready to move through. Tonight, he said he felt "well loved." He is, thanks to us all.

With much care, ~ Judy

Kim backpacking in Utah with old buddies Tejavani (Cheryl), Archie, and their daughter Sarah.

OCTOBER 31, 2007

Progress is moving haltingly forward. Baby steps, literally. Kim took a few teeny steps—which means putting weight on his LEFT leg. It's very exciting to know that there's some muscle tone there.

He also continues to eat well and is now cleared for nearly ANYthing that's relatively soft. Neighbors are treating him to wonderfully healthy organic foods made with love. Kim's drink of choice is sparkling water; he has traveled to Italy, Germany, and France through their finest. I, on the other hand, went to Mora's Ice Creamery today to buy the best I could find, and did—only to walk out without it! Ah yes, quite ditzy still. (Not to worry, I'll pick it up tomorrow.)

Yet I'm sobered tonight by the steepness of the path we're on. Although physical gains are made nearly daily, the psychic pain is huge. Kim is quite aware of what's going on and is grieving the loss of so many things. It's hard to know what he's thinking as he's a man of very few and quiet words these days. I try to imagine yet cannot. I do know that he will need every one of us to reflect back the strength we see in him, to help him find a way to be part of this new and brave world.

Thus, the days go by. Therapy takes up much of Kim's waking hours during the day; we are now plugged into somewhat normal meal times. I still think the best time to visit is right around dinner, 6:00 to 7:00. Other times are possible as well. Thank you so much for calling ahead, for it helps make sure Kim isn't overloaded as well and allows me to tell you if he's awake and up for company. Right now, there's not much more we need, just a bottle of bubbly and your good cheer. Archie and Cheryl are here all this week from Missoula and continue to be steady and cheerful support for us both. We remain so grateful for all.

With love, ~ Judy

Part 3
Moments of Connection

I have come to believe that what kept Kim tethered to this world in those first few tentative, tenuous weeks after his stroke, was connection. I held his hand nonstop; I sang to him every moment that I had enough breath; he heard the voices of his family and friends.

He was in a coma for much of that time, unable to respond, yet I noticed a flickering of his eyelids, tiny tremors in his breathing, subtle shifts of energy in his being. I became almost merged with that man (that never abated). I felt his tiredness, his hunger, his pain. I knew his energy. We were connected at the core.

Left to right: 1996, 2006, and 2010, three years after Kim's stroke.

'Twas a good thing, for there was a river of people who parted their busy lives to visit Kim and I needed to get skilled at setting boundaries; he had limited energy to invest. How lucky that Kim was quite the extrovert and happiest when being the center of attention, for people pulled him out. Always. Somehow he found a way to dive deep and bring up just enough energy to receive and greet.

I can still see his incredibly beautiful, profound eyes taking in everything, gleeful at the attention. His greatness showed through. As Rodney Smith, our Buddhist spiritual teacher, emphatically proclaimed, "Kim, you are not diminished!" Some things don't change.

November 4, 2007

I know it's been a while since I last wrote. Days run together, punctuated mostly by your cheery visits. Continued thanks for your flexibility and understanding as we navigate this unknown world. It's near impossible to plan when will be a good time to come by as we have yet to find a schedule for our days. Seeing you has been working out really well for us, and hopefully for you too.

Kim pulls together for these precious moments of connection. He very much wants to communicate as well as hear your stories. It does take a lot of energy for him, yet he rests better for it. I also know of the courage it takes for you to welcome this "new" Kim. I'm still learning who he is, and will be for a long while. He continues to go in and out of awareness, though his spirit is surprisingly strong. I do believe he feels deeply and is grappling courageously with what is asked of him.

Though there's nothing dramatic to report this week, Kim is making gains all around. Weight for one; he's put on 6 pounds! He manages to eat 2 out of 3 meals, with sleep being the limiting factor. Kim truly does enjoy food, eats thoughtfully, and comes out with the occasional "tasty."

He's more present, even playful, when awake, and he's definitely talking more and slowly getting his voice back. I miss Kim's exquisitely beautiful voice and have strong hopes that we'll sing together again.

I think I misled you when I said that he took "baby steps." He did put weight on his left leg yet needed much support to stand; he is not walking and may never—too soon to tell. PT and OT (physical and occupational therapy) work him hard: finding center and balance, learning how to move, working out painful kinks in his joints. Kim is always ready to try, ready to push through; he sets goals for himself every morning. Speech therapy is working on vocalizing and building up lung capacity, as well as assessing cognitive ability. We still don't know what his potential is for recovery. We hope to know within a few weeks when he'll be able to return to Harborview for their intensive rehab program.

On a playful endnote, Kim was a "spotty dog" for Halloween, as was our grandson in NY! He charmed the staff here. I love how the generations inspire each other. (Thanks to neighbor Chris Stanley for designing the costume, complete with ears fashioned from the compression socks he wore when at Island Rehab.) Also on that evening, the Wednesday night "Yurt Sangha" sat with us in quiet meditation; it was lovely and healing to bring that energy into the room.

Wishing peace for all, ~ Judy

P.S. As many of you have asked about me, please know that I am finding a way to sustain my energy. Yes, tired, yet also getting to the gym, eating well, and sleeping short but sweet nights at home with our kitty. Our friends are finding MANY ways to offer everything I could need. Once I see that Kim is able to push the "call" button and ask for help, I'll rest easier. Thank you truly for your care and concern; this IS hard.

November 5, 2007

I know that I just wrote last night but today was such a powerful day that I had to let you know. I am filled with hope.

For starters, Kim had a shower this morning—a rare treat. It is one of life's simple pleasures, yet how exhausting when you need to be transferred from bed to shower chair and back. I can tell that he loves the feel of water running over him.

It only got more dynamic from there. We had visitors from 10:00 a.m. 'til 8:00 p.m. this evening! He's remained gracious, welcoming, ready to play, and attentive to all, no exceptions. I'm no longer worrying about visits being too much for him; he thrives on your love and energy.

It's been a day of tripping down memory lane, from hiking in Peru in 1985 with David and Cynthia (who brought a stunning photo of Kim) to talking about witnessing human rights violations in Guatemala a few years back. He got teary reminiscing with his friends about the adventures they've shared, and I asked what he was feeling. "Joy," he said. I see how sadness carves out the heart to make room. And when Debra and Goyo acknowledged that what Kim is going through is hard, he responded, "Be assured that I welcome the challenge." Imagine that.

We also had a heartfelt conversation with our neighbor John about the meaning of life and what makes it worth living. Kim remembered that Morrie (of *Tuesdays with Morrie*) suggested that we have a memorial before we die to realize how loved and valued we are, sort of like what's been happening. There is no way to describe the power of your attention for me, too. I won't even try.

Nova commented that she wished she had half the resolve that Kim had. Kim said yes, he's determined. I'll only add that what makes him so exceptional to me is that his determination comes from love, not anger. His smile is more beautiful than ever, and our humor comes from a deep place of appreciation.

So yes, I am tired as it's late, yet I will sleep sweetly. Your prayers are working wonders and I thank you…

…With so much love and gratitude, ~ Judy

Kim befriending a young Mayan girl while working in the highlands of Guatemala, November 9, 2007.

Tonight marks 4 weeks at Island Rehab—hard to believe. It's good here, a healing place with excellent therapists and I love how close we are to home. Each day is packed full and no, never boring. Not that I can tell you all that transpires! I guess that's what happens when we focus on each moment…and we do, both of us.

There's been much progress this week. I know it cannot continue; yet it does. Kim is SO much more awake and alert, largely due to tweaking his drugs (less Dilantin, an antiseizure med). This impacts everything else and he now has that much more energy for therapy (up to 2 hours/day), and for eating—three 3 meals/day as of yesterday. His eyes tell everything: they are open, receptive, and BLUE.

Kim's also sitting straighter, righting his balance himself, gaining strength all around. He's in a new wheelchair and lookin' good. Kim talks of "dancing" with his therapists whom he appreciates so much. And in speech coaching (as he calls it), he found his deep bass voice yesterday for the first time. (Archie, wish you could hear it!) Now he's working on holding his "Aaaahhs" out longer. It's a lovely sound.

Having more of a voice means that he can chat on the phone and he did today, for the longest conversation ever I think, talking with his daughter Megan in NYC.

I was watching him from across the room and saw the sky roll across his face—smiling, crying, laughing. It's obvious to me that he feels all, fully.

We started reading Ram Dass's *Still Here* tonight. R. D. is the 1970s counterculture pioneer of *Be Here Now* fame who is still exploring new lands, this time writing about aging after his stroke. It's a beautifully written book by an inspiring mentor. He describes his wheelchair as his "swan boat" and notes how people of many cultures are honored by being carried and cared for. He speaks of how at peace he is right where he's at. "Healing does not mean going back to the way things were before, but rather allowing what is now to move us closer to God."

Acceptance. Kim has been grappling with integrating his left hand, frustrated that he cannot will it to move. By this evening he said he was befriending his left side, loving it, and fell asleep holding it tenderly with his right.

Yet some clear limitations are coming to light and, whether temporary or not, we don't yet know. So far, no ability to write—there's something missing between his intent and the action. "Simple" math and other cognitive skills aren't happening; seems that some of his rational abilities are/were located in his right brain. (Being left-handed mixes things up.) He looks at a toothbrush and wants to use it but can't quite put it together. We're still not sure what he can see.

This balances out what Kim excels in—being an even more expansive human being: loving, generous, playful, and kind. He greets everyone with his magnetic handshake, introduces people to each other, and thanks each person who enters his world for some "gift" they've given him. He seems to be happy, incredible as that sounds. There is a lot of laughter coming from our side of the room. We have the gift of no urgency, nowhere to go but right here and we are savoring the small things. So much of life is choosing what we pay attention to.

Kim is an absolute joy to be with and I feel honored to love him. As hard as the road is, I do trust that we can make it through everything with the support of our outrageously wonderful friends and family. Thank you for making asking for help so easy.

In peace, ~ Judy

NOVEMBER 11, 2007

Kim came home today. Just for a very brief visit—but oh! What joy, so much so. How incredible it is that we live half a block away from Island Rehab, no kidding.

We stopped first at the Common House, arriving just after our community's monthly meeting and found many people lingering. Perfect for us, for a circle formed around Kim and he greeted each person warmly—asked about their life, sent greetings to friends, and was his playful and loving self, including his new John Wayne voice. A wonder to behold.

We then made it home. Not an easy thing to do; I can scarcely imagine all that must run through his thoughts. We didn't stay long as he was tired, just long enough to pet Fuji (kitty extraordinaire) and get a scent and sense of the place he hasn't seen for nearly 2 months. Returning to his room, he said he was relieved. It is a safe place for him and that in itself is a comfort to me. I know why we're both so tired, with laughing and crying all mixed up.

This has been Kim's dream for a number of weeks now, and it's affecting him deeply. More tears as reality is setting into yet another level. He said we're in "sacred time," and we are. We cannot stay in the physical plane and find peace; we know that we are so much more than our bodies. He asked that I put his wedding ring, which I've been wearing around my neck ever since the stroke, on his right hand as his left is too swollen; I moved mine to my right as well. Tomorrow early morning we will reread our vows from 7+ years ago. We are so tightly connected.

Other details for those who want to know: Kim's dealing well with a wicked rash that's covering his body, most likely a reaction to the toxic level of Dilantin that was in his system. He still has headaches that make him wince and knee and hip pain that could be arthritis screaming at him. He seems to sail through much of the pain and doesn't hold onto it; when it's over he's ready for another story. (Take Garrett's story of losing his teeth at Petco—there are some great characters here.)

More soon. I'm amazed that the soups and breads and treats keep coming; I have yet to think about cooking. Your nurturing and cheer are carrying us along.

With love, ~ Judy

November 16, 2007

It's been a rainy and windy week here on Bainbridge, a good time to hunker down cozily at Island Rehab. And we are, doing well enough taking each day's challenges as they come, finding the humor and remembering to hold onto the long view.

Our brother-in-law, Kevin O'Brien from Massachusetts, left on Monday. His 5-day visit here was wonderful, for he brought a calm spirit and solid support for us both. I think that even he saw changes in Kim in that short time.

Highlights of the week:

- Kim has been standing a bit longer each day with help (it takes 2 to support him), yet I see it getting a bit easier. He's so motivated, works so hard.
- He's loving speech therapy. His voice continues to get stronger. I cherish his singing, and today he worked on *om mani padme hum*. Soothing and comforting to hear. "If you can talk, you can sing," and so we are.
- Kim is starting to write, or at least put pencil to paper. Not an easy thing as he may not see very well and he is using his right hand. It's awkward for him at best and great to see him wanting to learn.
- He's gained a few more pounds and is looking healthy. He commented that he's feeling "pretty beefy." Tube feeding is being cut back and will hopefully be ending before long.
- Yesterday Kim stayed awake all day, no nap in the afternoon. His energy continues to increase although his headaches continue to sap him and his rash is still distracting, to put it mildly. We're not sure what's up with that and have a consult at Harborview tomorrow. It's absolutely terrific to have him alert and communicative; he's very much the Kim I know and love.

As to what's next, today I learned from Harborview Rehab that they'd like to wait a few more weeks for Kim to get even stronger.

They believe in the quality of the therapists here on Bainbridge, as do we. Harborview only works with people for an average of 3 weeks at the tail end of their rehab, and it's best for Kim's to get as much daily therapy as he can before transferring there.

Debra, the lead therapist here, predicts that Kim will be able to transfer from bed to chair on his own and will not need round-the-clock care as I'd feared. Of course, everything can change, yet I'm grateful for these seeds of hope. Given all of this, we're looking at perhaps 5–6 more weeks before coming home. Could be a grrreat way to end the year.

We've been thoroughly enjoying our roommate of the past week, Sandy Cheryn. He's a drummer on the Island and has a great sense of humor, as well as many friends in common. We've had a bit of the party atmosphere in Room 19 with much laughter and a lot of coming and going of folks, making this a week of fun memories.

We've also been the recipients of some absolutely remarkable gifts—from a wheelchair nearly made for Kim (bought on eBay by an old Lummi Island friend Tom Stoesser)…to a Tibetan singing bowl (and another eve of shared meditation)…to a down sweater to keep Kim warm…handmade penguin pillow cases…books and CDs…a jar of oysters (a winning photo of Kim pulling them out and popping them into his mouth!)…NW jam and applesauce and soups…music…

and more. Two months in and you keep surprising us with your creativity and love, and we thank you. 'Tis truly a season of abundance.

Kim does shine for visitors, so please don't hesitate to contact me if you'd like to come by. Best times are weekdays between 4:00–8:00 and weekends. As each day is new, it helps us if you call before.

Lovely. Hope you are keeping warm and cozy.

We hold you in our thoughts and prayers. ~ Judy

November 19, 2007

Kim fell asleep smiling. I'm guessing that that must sound incredible to you, though as I have been in this drama for a while, I feel it too. He seems happy, truly—and we are. He is comfy and safe at Island Rehab, knows the staff, and has won over friends everywhere. He asks for therapy and is always up for working hard. He's gotten attached to his bed and now his chair; he so enjoys the food. We are easily amused and find many things very funny. Eating, for example, though it's hard to describe why. Kim is now feeding himself and most of it does make it to his mouth. Just imagine how he came up with the "Flying Fish Recovery Club."

We talked today with Greg Tuke, who just came back from a trip to India with his Bridges to Understanding program, working with youth in digital storytelling. He spoke of a project interviewing monks about what makes them happy. What a grand question! We were answering it too. Kim said that for him it's learning; for me it's being connected. We are in our element, for I cannot imagine a time when I have felt more connected, deeply so, to so many people…and Kim is growing and learning daily by leaps and bounds, almost literally.

Last night we made it to the West Sound Academy play. A simple sentence until one considers what that means. He got dressed in a new shirt, bundled up, and with Linn and Greg we wheeled down to the playhouse nearly a half mile away (taxi never showed up). At night. On sidewalks that all of a sudden seem rough and uneven. I had doubts; Kim was clear—he was going. Do not fear that his sense of adventure has diminished.

What a reception he received! He truly brings out the beauty in everyone and appreciates each person in turn. He was dignified and elegant, sitting tall in his chair, "cracked egg" and all (he now refers to himself as Humpty Dumpty). We didn't make it through the whole performance, but never mind. He reached his goal, as did I. He came home tired and cold yet excited and SO pleased. This felt like the beginning of our new life together and it feels good—it is real.

We also went to Harborview Hospital on Friday for a check-in with a rehab nurse practitioner. She clearly noted Kim's progress and reassured us that he's on the right track and the right meds. Again, not an easy trip, yet Kim sustained his energy all day and tolerated the discomforts without complaint.

I, too, am doing surprisingly well. Our room is a peaceful one, home for now and quite a joyful social scene. Thanks to friends I am getting (almost) enough rest and good, healthy food. Kim and I coined a new phrase today: "care receiver." We know about what it takes to sustain a "care giver." Yet we rarely talk about being the recipient of such care, a challenge unto itself—not something either of us have practiced much in our lives. And here we are, in a place where we must learn to accept gifts unending. It takes humility and a willingness to be vulnerable; it's another level of gratitude. I can say that it's a blessing, and I encourage all of us to put as much conscious energy into receiving as we do into giving.

So we start another week with something akin to excitement. Perhaps Kim will be close to standing soon and learning to pivot—the key for transferring from bed to chair and back. As of tonight he is totally unplugged; he's refused to take tube feeding any longer as he is eating heartily on his own. And today he had his first real hearty laughter, pure music to my ears, brought out by his old Lummi Island friend Pam. I think he enjoyed the sound of it as much as we did. Hallelujah!

Kim and I are learning that happiness is not about what we do or where we go but how loving we are in relationships, how open and curious we are about where we find ourselves, and how inventive we can be with what we're given. May we all fall asleep with a smile on our lips and lightness in our hearts.

In peace, ~ Judy

West Sound Academy students happily surrounding Kim.

Part 4
Radical Acceptance

There is much space and silence in our days. Kim needs time to gather up the spirit and energy to show up; I need the quiet to sort through and find my way back to acceptance.

I find that the slow pace of our days brings with it an unimagined richness. My senses are heightened: Colors take on deeper hues, sounds are louder, energy is tangible. I am more alive than ever.

We carve out extraordinary moments that bring such meaning to our days. From the late-night expedition to the West Sound Academy school play, to being honored for a lifetime of human rights activism, to making the harrowing trek to the library that he so loves, Kim is finding what brings him joy. And now with a wheelchair van, anything is possible. In spite of the roller-coaster ride, or perhaps because of it, we are accepting what is and savoring life.

November 22, 2007

Each day is new as Kim and I move deeper into recovery. My image, hard to explain, is that of peering intensely into a flower that keeps unfolding. More like petals that come into view as others drop off. No end in sight. Not unlike what I experience when I paint—when I see colors and shapes that were honestly not there when I started. It's a fascinating and rich time.

I wasn't going to write tonight, but here I sit! At Harborview today for a CAT scan and a date with the surgeons. They said "perfect." I think they were surprised at how good Kim looks, and is. The plan is for another check-in on December 26th and then surgery to put his skull back just after the holidays. They said it's a "simple" operation, that Kim would be kept just overnight. No way for me to understand it all, though I have come a long way toward keeping on breathing through bizarre images of what we can, and do, survive.

Kim's energy is nothing short of stunning. New records daily. Today he sat in his chair for 7 hours, rested in bed for another, then back up for an hour of intensive therapy. (He asked for it, couldn't imagine not working out.) He's talking up a storm and continues to be funnier than ever. Playful. A ton of fun to be around. Staff at Island Rehab are now taking their breaks in our room…he's eating well and enjoying such pleasures immensely. Used a "rocker" knife today to cut food. And there's promise of getting an extension on the left brake of his chair so that he can reach it with his right hand, which means that there's gonna be no way to keep that man still. (He's been joking about winning the "Octogenarian Special Olympics"; I only wonder aloud why he'd wait those many years.)

Yet, given all of this good news, the situation is outrageous to comprehend. I'm there, I'm IN it, and can only emerge to this reality slowly. To be grappled with in its own time. I think I'm aware of where we are, then I find myself shocked by how tall he is when he does stand, even when bent over. It's too much to take in, even in these two long months of witnessing and reflecting. It must be a powerful hit to someone who's just seeing Kim now.

Yet Kim remains beautiful and strong, unself-conscious and brave, open and curious. I have absolutely no idea how he does it. How does he manage to accept and to trust, and how is it that he focuses so totally on what he CAN do, not on what is no longer? The word that keeps coming to me is "summoned," as in "Kim has been summoned by a stroke." To what, I don't know.

You are remarkable too. Each of you brings a unique gift to us, be it a message or a poem, a story, or something comfy to eat or wear or look at or listen to. It seems to me that Kim is pulling out our highest selves. He must be resonating with exactly what we each need in order to become more whole, be it courage or clarity or kindness. I have no other way to explain the generosity and beauty that keeps flowing toward and around us.

So thank you once again. Here's to this season of gratitude and abundance. I'm really not as sappy and sweet as I fear I sound; my "other self" is alive and well too, I can report. Yet I remain happy and alert as we travel this path together, all of us. Truly, giving thanks.

Taking a long and deep breath with you, ~ Judy

NOVEMBER 27, 2007

We're into our 10th week, the 7th here on Bainbridge. Days run together and weeks fly by. We're falling into a bit of a rhythm, though I know it'll change soon.

Still no word on when we move back to Harborview; I'm guessing we're a few weeks out at most.

Kim continues to learn new things daily, like how to scooch himself up in the bed and grow adept at brushing his teeth (tonight, try it with your nondominant hand just for fun, forget the brain surgery part). He is so much stronger now and able to lean forward, reach over, and stand with assistance—all things that require good upper body strength.

He seems a bit more tired this last week, and his headache continues unabated. I wonder if Kim's fighting something, perhaps another UTI (urinary tract infection). I don't see myself as a worrier, I've just become so much more alert to signs of change. No doubt just the ups and downs of recovery.

I think I'm flowing with the current, but I've noticed how often I say "whoops." I'm aware that if I were truly relaxed and letting go of how I think things should be, there'd be no whoops-ing, so I've begun to count. I'm using "whoops" as my mindfulness bell. I'll let you know if I get anywhere.

At best, this progress puts us about 6 weeks out from returning home. But life has changed and our wonderful two-story home is no longer workable for us. Another loss, yet we've decided to move rather than go through the messy, expensive, and awkward business of remodeling. We have the unbelievable good fortune of moving into one of the 3 accessible units in our community that just happens to be available. Timing is perfect, to the month. It's a lovely home—open and light, with much sun and a large porch.

I cannot even make sense of how things like this happen. The chance of this working out would have seemed impossible before, yet here we are. I can only shake my head at how the world unfolds. No sense trying to rationalize any of it—it just is. I do think the universe has more magic and poetry in it than anything.

So to all of you asking, yes, we'll welcome your help! As we'll be downsizing quite a bit, I envision a blowout moving sale. We are thrilled, for leaving community was just not an option. We are indebted to our neighbors for so much, intricately and lovingly connected in such a tight weave that breaking it wasn't tenable. We would not be if it weren't for our community.

Our friend Kaaren just sent us this Rumi poem, fitting in more ways than one:

> *Sorrow prepares you for joy.*
> *It violently sweeps everything out of your house*
> *so that new joy can find space to enter.*
> *It shakes the yellow leaves from the bough of your heart*
> *so that fresh green leaves can grow in their place.*
> *It pulls up the rotten roots*

so that new roots hidden beneath have room to grow.
Whatever sorrow shakes from your heart,
far better things will take their place.

May I continue to trust the turbulence of this river we're in.

Warm thoughts to all on this cold night, ~ Judy

December 1, 2007

The Kitsap County Council for Human Rights has chosen us, as a couple, to receive the "Lifetime Achievement Award in Human Rights."

This is an unbelievable honor. I've been keeping it quiet this past week, turning it over like a stone in the river, amazed at the feel of it, trying to grasp what it means. Respect for all, no exceptions. Kindness at every turn. Advocacy and action woven into every day. I must say that the offering of it is heightening my intentions and efforts—"lifetime" meaning also from here on out. We'll be attending the Council's annual conference next Friday, December 7th, to accept this recognition humbly.

Along the human rights theme, we have our "Free Lefty!" ritual each morning. Lefty is Kim's left hand. (Anyone want to guess what he has named his right hand?) Every night he wears a brace to make sure his hand doesn't tighten into a claw; in the early morning it's our ritual for me to take off the brace and for us together to raise his arm high with a "Free Lefty!" cry. The best new news is that today there was the beginning of some muscle tone forming in his left arm. Too soon to say more, just that it's not as floppy as it's been.

As Kim is now so much stronger, transferring from bed to chair and back is getting easier. He's graduating from the "stork" sling that lifts him in a hammock to a machine that helps pull him to standing on his feet. He's nearing his full height, standing for short bursts of time, using his left leg, and holding his head high. It's a beautiful sight.

Kim also had his first "flush" this week. I won't go into too many details as we don't much talk about body functions in public. I'll just say that this is one of the greatest freedoms to achieve. Throughout all the ordeals, Kim maintains dignity and humor when others would crumble into embarrassment.

So tonight we turn another page of the calendar. It's a weird feeling to be in the same room most all day long for nearly 2 months now, watching the sun cross the sky a bit lower each day, noticing the change in the leaves and the temps getting colder, looking for a pattern in the birds that flit past our window. Same setting, different details. I'm learning that even when it seems that things aren't moving, they ARE. It's impossible to "step into the same river twice."

We're calm and steady. Now it looks like we'll be here at Island Rehab through the holidays. In early January his skull will be replaced, and then we'll head to Harborview Rehab. This puts us at coming home at the end of January, and yet I'm holding it all lightly.

Faith is a funny thing. It demands trust in the unseen. I need to renew it daily, still and always.

I'm grateful for your companionship as we move into the depths of winter.

With warmth and care, ~ Judy

December 8, 2007

Storms are raging outside while a tempest hit Kim this past week as well. Bainbridge Island got its share of flooding and winds while Kim was fighting not just another UTI but also a severe allergic reaction to the antibiotic he was on. It took us a while to figure it out as he was also started on a pain med the same eve and everyone thought his reaction was to that. Too, things move slowly here. Lordy. Scary to see him so lethargic again, not to mention the upset (literally) of his extreme sickness. I'm so pleased to say that he seems fine now, on yet another antibiotic and doing well.

On a high note, Kim's daughter Megan was here last week along with her partner Vincent and son Henry (who'll turn 3 on Monday). Her mother has been joining us as well, making the family whole. We're all closer than ever. It's never-ending fun to see how much Henry and his "Jempa Kimmie" are growing more alike—Henry noted that they are both in strollers, some bigger. Polly came too, of course—their happy Chihuahua who was in dog heaven cleaning up scraps of food from Kim's bed, floor, and bib. It's worth considering having such a dynamic Hoover.

Some news items:

- We are getting stronger, both of us. Stronger and better adept. We are now able, together, to get Kim from lying down to sitting at the edge of the bed. It may not sound like much but it's huge for us. The only downside is that we're not needing our wonderful aides and we miss them. So we call Garrett in for a good-night story, Rae to tell us a joke, Monica to whistle with Kim, and so it goes.

- Kim is totally unplugged now: His PEG tube (which was the line to his stomach for the feeding tube) was removed yesterday. A Declaration of Independence!
- Our favorite Harborview neurologist, Dr. Khot, saw Kim yesterday and seemed pleased. He tweaked Kim's meds to better manage the pain and reassured us that Kim still has a way to go in terms of healing and what strength he may regain. There is hope that Kim will be able to use the increased tone in his left side in some way, although it's too soon to tell.

And today Kim and I (and his sister Susie—so great to have her here) traveled to Bremerton where we were honored by the Kitsap Human Rights Council for our "extraordinary commitment to peace and human rights." Humbling and thrilling. Kim had the room totally silent while he spoke slowly and eloquently. His presence is great, and beautiful. Wondering where our paths are taking us…

Kim and his daughter Megan, Vincent, and grandson Henry about to set off on an adventure.

How funny to find that after a lifetime of activity, we are touching so many people just by being, doing nothing but making our way day by day. It's a magic I do not need to understand. I don't want to break the spell; all I can do is to just keep focused and attentive each moment. It's only when I forget that I lose it. Kim helps me stay in the present; we feed each other strength and energy and love, and tons of hope. We're happy.

Our friend and neighbor, Barbara, just sent me an exquisite bit on the violinist Itzhak Perlman, who miraculously played a stunning concert with only 3 strings when 1 broke. His explanation was, "You know, sometimes it's an artist's task to find out how much music you can still make with what you have left."

With cheer and love, ~ Judy

P.S. Mary, you're a riot! You got it. YES "Pancho" is Kim's right hand, though your Poncho story is the best ever. Time to sing…

Kim enjoying grandson Henry.

December 14, 2007

Life has a rhythm of its own. Each day is different, and each is packed with therapy x3 (physical, occupational, and speech), daily living activities (eating, washing, dressing) that take time and attention to detail, and wonderful visits from friends near and far. I can happily report that Kim is now off antibiotics as of this morning and done with infections. His headaches are so much better—much milder, much less frequent. I can now often see them coming and catch them before they blossom; I'm growing ever more in tune with Kim's needs. It's quite exciting to see him moooove with this freeing up of vital energy.

I was watching Kim experimenting with his wheelchair yesterday. As no therapist was claiming his time, he got restless and headed out to the hallway to practice steering straight. (We used to joke about "not having both oars in the water." It's a tribute to his humor that he can find that funny!) Forget demonstrating—he learns best by playing on his own. Kim's single-minded focus is a beautiful thing to witness, truly. Lasso his creativity, resourcefulness, intelligence, and motivation, and watch him move mountains.

Kim's strength shows up in many places. His ability to center himself for one, as his abs and trunk are gaining muscle. He's sitting straighter, and today he learned how to roll over in bed on his own—all this with only his right side shifting and maneuvering.

Then there's his spiritual strength. He tears easily, especially when thinking about old friends and things he used to do. He (and I) grieve almost daily, yet it passes and is quickly replaced by gratitude and joy. Believe it or not, today's sadness was over no longer being able to do hard work like wash dishes and scrub pots with his usual gusto! So, all ye creative friends, let's think up some good, hard, meaningful cleaning jobs for him. What an unusual man.

Kim is trusting me magnificently, and seems to be at peace with the way our lives are unfolding. It must take extraordinary faith to find oneself with so little control over one's life, over one's body. Kim said, "Faith + Trust = Love"; I added "+ Joy." Daily lessons and insights continue, and I find that I still need so much time to process it all. We decided that we were two secular Buddhists in divinity school.

We're holding to our timeline, planning to be at Harborview most of January and come home to our new place by February. I've also been handling moving, Medicaid, and financial matters, and am mighty grateful for folks helping me navigate these unknown and complex waters.

Your generosity continues undiminished. I still find food in our fridge when I come home late at night, still get instant responses to any requests I put out. I am stunned by the amount of time people are putting in to help us. Tremendous gratitude for our community flexing in creative ways to enable us to stay here, and a big bouquet to Marci for all of her hard work, attention to painstaking detail, and so much care.

In peace, - Judy

December 18, 2007

Hello Friends,

I won't wax too eloquently tonight as I promised myself to catch up on much-needed sleep—I just wanted to jot down a few things.

For one, there will be a dynamic concert happening on Bainbridge this coming Saturday, December 22nd. Billed as "Spirit of the Season" with some of the best local musicians and loveliest voices, it's also to be a fundraiser…for us! It's not our doing; our friend (and fellow mediator) David Hager proposed it. Our only sadness is that Kim and I will not be able to attend, both because getting out at night is difficult and also because we don't have a way to get there; wheelchair taxis don't run at night. I predict that it will be tremendously inspirational and inspired music, bringing together so many of our old friends.

As to adventures, we're only beginning to figure them out. Kim is talking of a trip to the coast (we'll soon be buying a van with a wheelchair lift), and in the meantime, we have plenty of pastures to explore close to home. Another great reason to live where we do, with so much within wheeling distance.

Yesterday it was a trip to the library, a touchstone for Kim. It was getting into the late afternoon before we mobilized; the weather was grey and "spitting." We started out by singing under the gazebo in the back garden, but then Kim wanted to get to the road, and he then set his sights on the library about 4 blocks away. I've never paid so much attention to how driveways are cut into sidewalks. I'm learning the difference between the older ones (that tilt chairs) and the newer versions that just dip. I'm getting stronger.

We made it, and Kim took out a book on tape (the Dalai Lama's *Advice on Dying and Living a Better Life*). But when we bundled up to return home, it was not just raining buckets but windy too. We had little choice. I happened to have an umbrella, a bright blue and silver one we'd bought in South Africa, and off we went. Quickly. Must've been a sight with Kim in his blue down jacket, blue helmet, and bulky wine-colored blanket across his legs, holding onto this umbrella Mary Poppins-style. He loved it, as did I. Just a little edgy.

Yet today was a challenge, as the new longer-lasting pain med tried on Kim last night didn't agree with him: another morning of monstrous headache, nausea, and fatigue. He was better by this eve, but oh, it doesn't get any easier for either of us. (For those who've asked, I do have my bouts of the "fall-aparts" as in today, not always a pretty sight.)

But just to leave you with a bit of humor as I seem to need to, here are a few images:

- Coming out of the shower Kim was draped in towels and thick sheets. I called him my "sheik," but he heard "sheep" and asked if I was Bo Peep.
- Kim chuckling today imagining "a brain-damaged humanities teacher with double vision trying to parallel park." I'm sure that doesn't sound very funny, but to see him get a kick out of the absurdity of it all is quite heart-rending and poignant. If he finds the humor in that, how can we not?

So yes, we continue to accept what's given to us with as much surrender as we can muster and give every ounce of strength, determination, focus, and joy on what we CAN affect. Wishing you the same.

Sending warmth and cheer as we head into the darkest days of the year.

With love, ~ Judy

Journal writing on a train in Zambia, perhaps penning a poem.

December 23, 2007

As the concert was starting in Rolling Bay, Kim fell asleep to my singing "Home of My Heart"—a most beautiful, soulful song taught to us by our 13-year-old friend Linnaea. I love it when music can soothe Kim's brow, often fretted with the strain of a headache or fears unknown to me. He's well-covered by a thick, gilded quilt sewn by Joanne, a cloth version of Van Gogh's starry-night café scene. He's breathing peacefully and evenly as I write this.

I'm thinking of our friends who are, right now, being treated to the harmonies of David and Jennifer Hager, Emily Groff, and Ian Turner. From where do these kindnesses come? These musicians are turning their talents into a gift for us, and we thank all of you. I am happily "tuning in" to the warmth and the exquisite harmonies radiating out.

Lyrics from a song I learned long ago: "Song fills up the soul, soul opens the heart. The heart welcomes the light. Banish the night with song." A perfect reminder for this long, dark winter solstice night.

We've had a tough week as a third UTI has blossomed in Kim. He's holding up as best he can, but the infection saps his energy at a time when he needs these precious weeks to gain strength. Yet I see him learning—better adept at recognizing patterns visually, reading slowly (maneuvering through distorted spatial perceptions), beginning to write (made it A to Z this week), and he seems to enjoy taking pen to paper and doodling. I have plans of some creative visual storytelling over the holidays.

When the first wave of holiday cards came, I was sure that people were really pushing the season early. So much for my tracking events outside this room! By now we have dozens gracing our walls. How can this be? Tomorrow marks the end of month #3 since Kim's stroke, and the flurry of your messages, cards, and gifts has not let up. I have the sincere intention to respond to each, though realistically I may not make it until Groundhog Day.

Yet please know that we hear every word you say and send. I read to Kim daily (and now he's reading many himself!). We sit silently after each note, often in tears, remembering friends, recalling shared moments. I cannot exaggerate how important you are to us.

In lieu of a gift, here are a few images to add some holiday cheer:

- Kim was geared up, helmet and all, about to stand at the parallel bars when he put up his hand to stop the 3 (three!) therapists ready to support him. He needed first to take a drink of water and said, "Evel Knievel takes a sip of his favorite beer before a stunt."

- Megan, Kim's daughter, designs clothes. The two of them were working on a new line for the "fashionably disabled," including monogrammed Depends.
- Jon came by last night bearing one of Kim's all-time favorite treats: the sensual smell of the sea captured in a jar of oysters. With that and challah, we welcomed the Sabbath and toasted to the turning of the season. L'chaim! To life!

To life and light and love, ~ Judy

P.S. The Kim Bush Fund (now a special needs trust) continues to be attracting amazing support. Yes, checks to "Kim Bush Fund" or "Kim Bush Trust" are so very, very appreciated. I have some work to do around understanding and accepting this kind of financial generosity. If money is energy, we must be getting ready for some bright burning! It will be our manna-from-heaven, and we thank you.

DECEMBER 28, 2007

Hello Friends and Family,

'Tis the season to keep you even closer to us in our hearts, and we are. We did have a bit of snow on Christmas Day, which was festive and lovely, although with the rain today, our 3-year-old neighbor Theo said he was catching drops of "snow" on his tongue…the NW version of the white stuff.

Kim had the energy, so we rolled to Cohousing that morning for some singing and munching. It moved us both to just be home again, surrounded by friends who continue to stand by us. As it had started snowing when we left, about 15 folks decided to accompany us caroling all the way back with umbrellas held high over Kim's head and mine. It's hard to describe the full regality of the scene—could've been an old-time picture postcard. VERY sweet.

We've also been treated to visits from my cousins Jon and Rose from Santa Rosa, who bring wonderful memories of our shared times, as well as Megan's 4th visit from New York City in the last 3 months! She somehow found time to make us Christmas stockings and more. For those observant folks who are able to come by Room 19, you might notice that all of the cards now hanging on the wall are new ones. We're happily buried in warm holiday wishes from you.

The news. Although Kim's UTI is waning, he had a cold earlier this week and now I'm smitten. Doing well enough through the sniffles. Harder, is that our visit to the surgeon yesterday gave us the news that our hoped-for surgery next week is postponed, perhaps by as much as 2 months. They are concerned about infection and said that Kim's incision isn't healing perfectly. Quite a different take on it than the last resident gave us a month ago. We'll check in again in a month from now to see how things look.

Yes, disappointed for sure, yet we agree with being safe (of course). As so many people are gone this week, we'll wait 'til next to talk with the therapists and see if we can go ahead with plans to go to inpatient rehab in Seattle in mid-January, although the skull replacement won't happen 'til after those 3 weeks. Though I think I'm holding things lightly, it's a wake-up call to see my spirits take a dive when things change. I'm definitely wanting some semblance of control over our lives or at least a bit of predictability, and that's not happening.

Yet today was another historic day, as I bought a van! Yup, a new van, brand-new, and large for us: a Toyota Sienna that's been made wheelchair-accessible. Like magic: it has a dropped floor, "kneels" when the side door opens and the ramp folds out, and boasts a whopping 5' headroom inside. It's quiet, it purrs, it's smooth. All quite a shock after our 1989 Honda. I cannot wait to see Kim sitting in the passenger seat looking out on a green world passing by. Sunroof too, and I'm thrilled for the light. Couldn't have done it without Chuck's support and company: His unbridled joy in shopping and his patience while I wrestled with such new "firsts" made this all possible. So watch out! Kim is ever an adventurer and we're bound to show up on your doorstep before too long.

As Kim and I look back on the crests and troughs of this last year, we choose to focus on our blessings and trust that we will make it well through the challenges ahead. We are safe, we are loved, and we are surrounded by your prayers.

Sending so much cheer and warmth to you, ~ Judy

Hiking with cousins Jon and Rose; we loved the mountains.

January 3, 2008

I was hoping to write next when I had a clear date for inpatient rehab at Harborview, surgery, or ANYthing, but alas, no such luck. Each day is ever-new and unpredictable and try as I might, I cannot pin anything down. Guess I'm still needing lots of practice on how to let go and trust timing. My! This is testing me for I'm so ready to have Kim come home and figure out how we can create a life together again. Patience; it's time to quiet and breathe.

Yet I wanted to let you know that we had our first ride in the "Silver Camel." (Kim named our van for its kneeling ability.) Kim looked absolutely elegant sitting tall. Headed to the water, of course, with Jon who shares our love for the smell of the sea. It was a beautiful, calm day. We wheeled Kim down the floating dock, over the rough cracks, and around the pilings. He joked about going swimming, but the width was just enough. We love the feel of the water beneath, gently lifting us. He said, "Mama Poseidon has us in her briny embrace."

Other great news is that Kim has taken a few steps. With support for sure, yet there he was standing 6'3" and putting all of his weight on his left leg. Even lifted his right in a great blue heron pose. Muscle tone is kicking in, and it just may be that someday he'll be able to use his left leg. This is emotional stuff.

Yet Kim still has a UTI and they are looking for another antibiotic to tame it (he's grown resistant to the last). His severe headaches continue. He's managed to not lose weight, yet he hasn't gained any either, although we're trying. Reading or writing is very exhausting, even painful for Kim, as it seems he cannot see very well at all. I've been falling prey to fear, allowing the what-ifs to speak. Kim has been steadying me, asking to "let our love sustain us, like breath."

So I turn to the belly of the sea, the birds that never quit, the winds that blow through and rearrange things, and to imagination and play and humor, knowing that this time of immense change will also pass. Back to remembering that I can only be present right now and welcome what is. I see us practicing daily, helping each other through the rough patches, not looking back with regret but rather being grateful for today. No one said it was gonna be easy.

So yes, I will let you know when we know what's up next. I'm still envisioning (holding lightly) being in our new home close to the end of this month. Although I'm not always talkative when you call or come by, please know that your care is THE critical link that helps us keep perspective and cheer. We are ever-hopeful and very ready for the new year.

Peace and ease to you too, ~ Judy

CAMEL ENVY

by Kim Bush

I've lost my lover to a camel…
no, to three of them.

I, a clumsy cowboy,
squirming in my saddle —

stirrups akimbo-
ache to win her back.

Galloping as fast as I can
I whip Raju with a willow stick

and imitate the clucking sound
that urges him to move.

I'd settle for a simple smile,
even a token gesture,

but the desert and its family
hold her in their sweet embrace.

January 11, 2008

I've been feeling like I'm a sailboat at sea. Not lost, as I'm not far from land and can see where I want to go. Yet I cannot quite seem to get there. Tossed wildly by the winds that come out of all directions, unpredictable and harsh. I start to tack but soon as I set sail, I get sideswept by yet another gust. Nor can I set anchor, for it's too deep here. Best I can figure is to hunker down and wait, taking deep breaths, trusting that the winds too will calm, the sky will clear, and the way will open.

Maybe it did today. Outside it was that timeless grey that doesn't much inspire, yet in Room 19 we got word that we're to head to Harborview on Monday. Lordy, are we ever ready for the change! Although as soon as I say that, I want to take it back, recognizing that today is what we know now, this day we've been given and it's good.

It's been fascinating to witness my moods: many cloudy moments, rain often, and momentary brightness but also strikes of lightning. I'm watching how my wanting other than what I have—to be elsewhere—pulls me out of center. Resting in the moment. What a challenge, for without also moving toward the future we would not have a new home to return to. (Work on the new unit began this week; it looks like the remodel will be ready in time.) Kim's working on physical balance and I on this one, both of us standing tall.

So much for the color of this past week. The drama is that we've had some more adventures as well as setbacks. Went in the Silver Camel to the movies on Saturday and just loved it. Neighbors Marci and John joined us. What grand fun to hear Kim's laughter ring out, see him eat popcorn with gusto. We were happily entertained. We're getting more adept at moving around: it's as easy to head out for a spin around the block as it is to pile into the van. He's talking the coast; I'm up for finding some snow and high vistas; he's mentioned Mazatlán!

What makes all this thinkable is that we are beginning to transfer. That means that we, together, will be able to move him from bed to chair to toilet and back again without a lift machine (which is what we've been using). Very exciting as this is THE missing piece. This takes so much courage, balance, strength, and trust on Kim's part. He's trusting me and I'm learning to use my body to balance his weight.

There are setbacks: a new antibiotic and upset stomach coupled with severe pain and intensive workouts that demand equilibrium. He's had the last of the difficult injections, although we don't yet know if the UTI is gone. We're sincerely hoping that Harborview will offer us the kind of medical care that can help us kick this infection in the you-know-what.

So perhaps my next missive will be from Harborview. Please wish us well. We hear that Harborview is one of the top rehab places in the country, that it is "boot camp." Kim revels in that though it's bound to test us both. Best possible scenario is that after 3–4 weeks of therapy, he'll be well enough to have the surgery to replace his skull…which puts us home by early February.

And please keep Kenya in your thoughts too. The violence there is painful to imagine.

Thanks for your care, your support, and your love, ~ Judy

January 16, 2008

It's wonderful to be here. We landed at Harborview's inpatient rehab unit yesterday afternoon. Today was Kim's first day and it WAS a full one with some 4 hours of speech, occupational, and physical therapies. We also spoke with a recreational therapist who sounds optimistic about getting Kim on the water and perhaps on a bike as well! There's so much to look forward to.

We're in a different world. There's a daily schedule written up on a white board and we work with the same therapists every day. The attending and resident docs come in daily to check in; nurses and aides are quite available. It's absolutely exciting to be among others intent on getting stronger. Kim's bed is comfy (fits his 6'3" frame) and it's so much quieter and calmer here. We watched the sunset over the water from our window this evening; I wheeled Kim to where the orange glow lit up his face. He looked radiant.

Other good news is that his UTI seems to be gone. I say "seems" only because I'm afraid to believe it. Yes! One more major hurdle behind us.

We have so much to learn: about Kim's vision and how to prevent the headaches that inevitably come from his efforts to read and write…getting smoother at transfers…ways for Kim to become more independent with daily living activities such as dressing and bathing. He'll be getting a lighter wheelchair now that he's better able to sit straight on his own. And there's talk of Kim working on the computer, perhaps with voice-activated software. We'll learn so much more about what's out there to help make life easier.

As we leave Bainbridge for this exceptional opportunity, I do want to take a moment to acknowledge the staff at Island Health and Rehab who cared so much for Kim and really made our 3+ months there a healing time. And I cannot say enough about our friends and neighbors. I don't think Kim was alone for more than an hour at a time; so many people came to sit with him so that he would feel accompanied. I must believe that that comfort and contact has played a huge part in his recovery.

My best guess is that I'll be commuting home a few times a week this next month. Visitors are welcomed on weekends and maybe evenings once Kim gets used to this demanding schedule. Feel free to call me on my cell, although I cannot always answer it or return calls quickly. I'm sorry, for it's hard to turn away friends who want to say hello. I can only say that it takes so much energy for Kim to stay focused and present. He is drained by evening, for his migraines continue; hopefully that will ease as he adapts to being here. Please know that we do love your care and will look forward to catching up soon.

In case you haven't already been to this website, do check out www.kimbush.net. Greg MacDonald, a fellow teacher at West Sound, put together some very delightful pictures of Kim. As soon as I can wrap my head around this technology, I hope to add some recent ones as well.

Our best to you all. May this next month be an enriching one for us all, a time of positive change. (Buds are beginning to come out, in January!)

~ Judy

January 22, 2008

We have our first full and memorable week behind us. After the initial days of adjusting to everything being new, Kim is managing to work his magic in connecting with the staff. That alone is exciting, for Harborview is such a diverse place with people coming from Korea, Vietnam, Tibet, India, Ethiopia, Tanzania, Russia, and more, just for a start. You might imagine how Kim asks about each place, happily listening to stories and delighting people with how much he knows about the world.

His therapy schedule remains demanding. Kim starts at 9:00 a.m. and is usually done by 3:00 p.m., and sleeping every chance he gets in between. Yet his improvement is already noticeable: standing taller and easier, transferring well, and growing more independent and comfortable all around. Leslie, his speech therapist, is right on, pulling out all sorts of maps to entice Kim to read. The world map was his "carrot" today for working hard. He's trying out a new streamlined chair today he calls his "Peugeot." It's wonderful to watch him better able to maneuver. Kim's sleeping better too, as they have given us a palatial single room with space enough to stretch out.

The team approach here is exemplary. Each week we meet with his attending doctor, main nurse, the physical-occupational-speech therapists, a neuropsychologist, and a social worker. Kim sits at the head of the table with all listening to his input and questions, each in turn speaking of their goals for him.

Our discharge date is set for Saturday, February 9th. Of course, things may change, although it's a great to have a guideline to hold onto. Not yet sure about the surgery; we may learn more this week. I must admit to being mighty hopeful, happily envisioning being home s-o-o-n.

All's going well on that front too. Our new place is in the process of being remodeled; it will be ready for us in time. I plan to find a few days when I can be on the Island and will ask for help moving some furniture over from our old unit.

There's really not much we need right now. Kim is well cared for and I'm staying here most nights. We love seeing friends, yet visiting times are limited while he's here (Sundays are still best, with possible afternoons/eves).

Thanks for keeping us in your thoughts and heart. Let's stretch these glorious sunny days and remember that spring is not far away.

With good cheer, ~ Judy

January 30, 2008

I've been reading *The Diving Bell and the Butterfly* to Kim each night before he falls asleep. It's written by Jean-Dominique Bauby, editor of the French magazine *Elle* who, at age 43, had a stroke that left him completely paralyzed. The only way he could communicate was by blinking his left eye. Absolutely incredible, poignant, difficult, and yet surprisingly uplifting. We close the book each night feeling utterly grateful; I do not know who I would be if Kim couldn't communicate, let alone so beautifully.

And he does! Tonight he was especially funny and I am SO pleased at his increased energy. He's been mighty fatigued these last few weeks; today seemed to be a turning point. He kept up with his therapy, including going to a group for people with traumatic brain injuries. I play with envisioning a time when Kim doesn't have headaches or constant pain and has the energy to access his adventurous self. It's there, for sure, just often beneath the surface.

Our lives keep turning. It's been a rough few weeks. I especially miss being close to home with the support of friends nearby. Too, I'm juggling being present with Kim while also managing logistics for our move and figuring out what we'll need in this next chapter, from people-help to bed and chairs. It is all coming together, and I'll bet that timing is perfect.

Our discharge date is being pushed back, for we now have a date for Kim's surgery. It's been a wild stop-n-go ride, yet the lead surgeon came by yesterday and confirmed that Kim is indeed ready for the procedure. I'm really pleased, as I believe having his skull back will greatly help his ongoing headaches, his feeling whole, and will reduce the chance of damage to his vulnerable brain. Too, I am relieved to know that we'll have round-the-clock attention and care during this time. Yet the surgery also will require quite a bit of strength and courage on Kim's part, and though they call it "simple," it's hardly a small thing to add to all that he's carrying.

As of today, it looks like next Friday, February 8th, is the date for surgery. There's talk of a return to rehab after that. It'd terrific to be given more coaching, although we don't yet know how long that could be. So no, we're not sure when we will truly be home. Deep breaths to us all.

Our good friend Jon spoke to us a few weeks back of how all mystical, magical stories have a part where there's a narrow bridge or sharp precipice to cross and we have a choice of moving forward in fear or taking steps in faith. I do teeter, yet I try to pay attention enough to stay on the side of trust. Your care and words of encouragement are often the extra support I need to steady me. I read the Message Board for spirit-food and thank you so for journeying alongside us so caringly.

With love, ~ Judy

Bird-watching with friends in Kenya.

February 4, 2008

HELLO FRIENDS:

Ready for my voice?

Judy has spoken for us beautifully.

We are thriving here as a team.

I'm getting stronger with this coaching and my confidence grows apace. See, your good thoughts and prayers are bearing fruit!

Thank you for your mettā, generosity, and care.

Love, Kim

Kim welcoming everyone outside our door in Winslow Cohousing.

Part 5
Music Heals

Kim's voice no longer has the resonance it once did, yet it is music to my ears. In fact, it is strongest when he sings! How grateful I am that he didn't lose his voice, his humor, or his wit. He continues to exert his unique spirit of play and kindness and can make his wishes known.

After nearly five months of hard work in rehab, we are about to come back to our community, to a new home. There are fresh challenges to which to adjust, yet the joy and quiet of a "normal" life is thrilling. The impossible just takes a little longer.

And yet, this is tough. Tougher, I think, than anything I've ever done. It's true that I tend to write only when I have the space in my thoughts to reflect on the days gone by. I find that I go to the natural world for my healing, for my solace. The vastness and beauty of the elements continue to soothe and teach me, especially the embrace of the watery world and the music of birds.

February 10, 2008

How we love your messages! Truly, I could not exaggerate how important your words are, knowing that so, so many in our circle of friends and family are celebrating the small successes with us and holding us close when things are tough. THANK you.

YES, we're on the other side of surgery. Phew. Kim went in last night around 6:00 p.m. and he's looking good today. Pain is lessening by the hour. It is HIS skull that they took out of the freezer (in time, to my relief) and the surgeons say that it fits perfectly. It's terrific to see him "well-rounded" again, and there is lots of hope that his headaches will abate. Too, we now have a sky-blue helmet with nothing to do as his brain is again protected. All thrilling and terrific.

Yet we're not home-free. Tonight, just 24 hours after surgery, his heart went into atrial fibrillation again (very fast and arrhythmic): Blood pressure is low, pulse is wild. No doubt it's a combination of the stress of surgery, having his meds tossed around a bit by all that's going on, not sleeping for a few days, and more. We just got moved to yet another floor where his vital signs can be monitored 24/7. He's getting the best of care. I really have no idea what's in store; the hope is that his heart will return to sinus rhythm with no surprises. Again, I can say how grateful I am that we are here at Harborview, the trauma center of the NW.

I also have to accept that he is in an extremely vulnerable place. His chance of having another stroke is very real. I just drop to the earth, breathe slowly and quietly, and then dive deep into waters where things are calm and steady. From there I can handle anything.

There's so much more I could say, and will, when I have the space and time. Please forgive me for not writing more. My days are full and all-consuming. What I can say, easily, is that Kim continues to work wonderfully hard and does not mire in self-pity or self-consciousness. His delightful imagination and humor stay strong. He is so loving and gracious that I find companioning him an honor and a joy.

With faith, ~ Judy

FEBRUARY 13, 2008

I'm just giddy with relief and hope. Kim is SO much better, yet another miracle. Yesterday, only 4 days after surgery, he had a full day of therapy and forgot to ask for pain meds in the evening. How can this be? I shall not question it, just enjoy it.

Yes, his heart went back to sinus rhythm (steady beat) just a few hours after going into AFib on Saturday. Really, this place knows how to jump into action. We returned to the rehab floor on Sunday. Kim slept most of Monday but did get in his chair in the afternoon, and by Tuesday he was back to his old routine. Nurses and therapists keep stopping by to meet the "new" Kim. He continues to charm people with his calm and gentle being.

If you (if I) can believe this, we are scheduled to come home (BOTH of us) on SATURDAY! No joshing, just 2 days after Valentine's Day. I can scarcely conceal my joy. Still lots to do at our new "sun home" before then to make it welcoming, but I no longer get anxious about such things. There is a whole world of magic and elves surrounding us who just seem to make things happen. (I can also say that the amount of money that found its way to Kim's Trust Fund equals, if not exceeds, the amount we've spent so far on medical bills and making our home accessible.)

So yes, life really is as good as it sounds. We're laughing, we're happy, and we're beginning to dream about our new life together outside of a hospital. After spending 4½ months in a small room, our home will seem spacious indeed. We're talking of joining the community Tree Frog chorus …Kim has been accepted to be on the Bainbridge Island Library Board and I on the Multicultural Advisory Committee for the school district…we are looking at getting involved in raising awareness about disabilities, especially with youth…and we cannot wait to get back involved with our community. Our home will always have an open door and an extra bed, the teakettle on, and something baking in the oven. Please find us.

NOTICE: Our wonderful friend Cassie Gleckler is putting together yet another musical event for us, a "Gypsy Jazz" concert on March 15th. Please find her message on the Message Board and come if you can. We do hope to be there as well and are grateful for her creativity and energy.

I'll end with a few unique Kim-erisims for fun. Hope they bring smiles to you too.

- Kim is aware that he tends to drool out of the left side of his mouth. He's not self-conscious about it; he just always wants to make the best of things. His latest idea is to call it a "drool irrigation zone" and put a planter on his lap with catnip to lure our kitty Fuji there.
- One of my concerns about going home is that Kim will expect the kind of variety and meat-filled meals he's been getting here. He loves the food and has asked if Harborview has a cookbook. He loves the lentil soup especially. The look on the nutritionist's face was priceless!
- At one meal he stared down at his lasagna, then quietly said he'd use lasagna as an object for meditation.
- One day at Speech Group where others with brain injuries meet to work on conversation, the facilitator asked each person what their middle name is. It was Kim's turn. He tends to speak slowly and thoughtfully. It was taking him longer than usual to answer. Now I know that he doesn't have a middle name, so I was curious what he was thinking about. He finally said "Burly." Out of respect, the others nodded seriously, trying it on…until they saw me laugh so hard the tears were running. Of course! KimBERLY!

Never ceasing to amaze me, touch me, and find a way to pull out the belly laughs. I know that Kim's remarkable healing (and mine) continue to sail along on the winds of your love. Sending bouquets and hearts to you all, and deep bows. Tomorrow will truly be a Valentine's Day to celebrate.

We love you, ~ Judy (and Kim)

February 23, 2008

It's all true. Kim graduated from Harborview Prep after 5 weeks of intensive rehab and we're now nestled in our home. Incredible!

We love being here. Our new place is beautiful and cozy, and the community is wonderfully welcoming—as well as exceptionally kind and sensitive to our needs. We were greeted by a cheerful sign and huge kid-made valentines taped to our door, chalk drawings of hearts and flowers on the walkway, and tulips gracing our home. People keep gifting us with food and cheer, sharing cups of tea. Our sweet kitty Fuji weathered 5 months of us being gone and seems so happy, still up to her old tricks. I do believe she's psychic as she's definitely doting on Kim. It's a tribute to my growth that I'm pleased by that (right?).

We are soaking up the sun. No joshing; ever since we landed here, it's been uncommonly beautiful. We even picnicked on our deck yesterday with Megan and Henry and Judy. Beaucoup windows face south and west, something we sorely lacked where we lived before. How healing. Megan calls this our "tree house" as we have windows all around and are high above the cars below. I even turned a few spadefuls of dirt today and am dreaming of all I can plant. We are contented and peaceful.

Also true is that adjusting to being on our own is a new challenge all its own. I am learning to live on very little sleep as Kim needs to be turned every 2 to 3 hours all through the night. He cannot be left alone at all, so a high priority for me is to find caregivers who can handle all sorts of possibilities. I hope to be able to find a rhythm that will work. We've been practicing with walkie-talkies for those moments when I'm in the Common House or down at our old home moving, inviting some pretty funny conversations between us. There is still a lot to do to get ready for the new family moving in.

We have a home health nurse as well as physical and occupational therapists coming here to work with Kim for a few weeks until they decide we're ready to go to being outpatient for that kind of support. And we do have many follow-up dates with docs at Harborview over the next few months. No lack of attention. Kim continues to heal well and is holding his own.

There has hardly been a quiet moment. And when there has been, I've slept, thus my silence in writing. I apologize. Too, our Internet connection here is still intermittent, though I'll try to check email frequently.

I am in awe with how things have come together for us. Bathroom has been completely remodeled to be accessible, rooms have been painted, kitchen cabinets are in, friends have helped move furniture, and our bed is working out well enough. If ever I doubt, I remind myself of the serendipity of this home being available at exactly the right time for us to be here. Our gratitude has not diminished. We find lots to laugh about, balancing out the tough moments. Great acknowledgment for me today when Kim said that I had "firewoman mentality."

Kim continues to awe me with how he handles the immense changes in his life. I weep when I go back to our old home and see all the things from bicycle to boat, books, and more that he will most likely never do again. Yet his tears are most always "tears of joy" as he calls them, not grief. I know he's searching for ways to contribute meaningfully, things he can do. He talks of carving stone, for one. We'll work hard on community involvement and creative outlets.

Again, we invite you to come by and visit, stay for a while. I am ready to bake and music is happening; we've been singing! Pulled out my guitar today and we let 'er rip. Please help us make this place a home.

May we all bask in the springtime sun and sweet air.

With love and thanks for your care, ~ Judy

MARCH 4, 2008

We're now into our 3rd week at home, happily nestling into this sunny tree house. I see signs of Kim relaxing: sleeping a bit better, comfortable in his recliner, enjoying folks stopping by…and I've been baking, putting in a few plants, and sharing priceless moments with neighbors. We're slowly reconnecting with our Cohousing community, back to sharing meals and work, and picking up where we left off last September. It feels grrreat.

Our days are full, although I'm hard-pressed to explain why. Home Health sends us physical-occupational-speech therapists as well as a nurse, twice a week each. They will continue for another few weeks, then Kim heads to outpatient therapy, most likely at Island Rehab where we were last fall. He is making small gains in finding his center and sitting straighter, taking in his left side and left field of view. Still has no use of his left arm and hand although his left leg does kick in (literally) when I do morning exercises with him. No one can say where any of this will lead as each person is so differently "stroked," not to mention the 3 brain surgeries he's survived. Yet Kim continues to amaze me with his presence and clarity, his stunning memory, improved hearing and sense of smell, and his playful, loving humor. He wastes no time on self-pity.

A more difficult challenge is what he calls his "gyroscope." Probably set off by poor vision and perception, Kim gets dizzy when moving from prone to sitting and when riding in the Silver Camel, even for short distances. So much for trips of any kind right now, though we do have weekly visits to Seattle for docs. We'll soon consult with an ophthalmologist for advice.

We did make it to the movies last week to see *The Diving Bell and the Butterfly*, a beautiful and heart-wrenching rendition of the book we had read last month about a man whose stroke left him completely paralyzed except for his left eye. At times tender, at times angry and regretful, it provided a backdrop for our drama and left us grateful for how much we do have—our continued theme, a critically important one.

I'm also focused on finishing the move from our old home and finding help with caregiving. It's been surprisingly tough to locate a person and/or an agency that can offer this level of care for 2–3 hours a few days a week. I am pleased that we are able to manage this well alone, yet I would be so grateful for the chance to take care of things I've long put on hold. Late yesterday I spoke with an agency that may pan out.

Probably the best way to reach us is our home phone as my cell doesn't work well here and email is intermittent. Please keep us in your thoughts and hearts as we make it through this transition period, for your good energy and kindness continues to sustain us. (As do the gifts of food friends bring by!) We are amazed by the generosity surrounding us. I trust that we will soon begin to define a life that includes increased community involvement and giving back, more music, and creativity of many expressions.

Take note: Cassie is now putting up flyers for a "Community Celebration for Kim" the eve of Saturday, March 15th with gypsy jazz violin and more foot-stomping music. She's posted info on the Message Board; please check it out and join us if you can.

Our door is always open and the teakettle is on. Bird feeders are up and the word is getting out to our feathered friends. Do stop by and add warmth to our cozy nest.

Blessings to all. ~ Judy

MARCH 12, 2008

A few days ago, I was tempted to write an update saying that I wouldn't be writing too much more as we were beginning to get the hang of being home and managing daily living—not very dramatic and newsworthy. It felt like life was becoming just a bit more predictable, even if we didn't yet have a steady routine.

But on Sunday, Kim had a seizure just before we were to dive into French toast lathered in syrup and peach yogurt (bad timing, said the ER nurse). It was his first seizure. It didn't last more than a minute and Kim recouped quickly, but it was sobering nonetheless. I did call 911, our incredible response system. We were swept up in an ambulance and taken to Harborview; we surely didn't expect to see the inside of that hospital this soon. I now know the difference between a seizure (electrical activity) and a stroke (blood clot in the brain), and how they show up. I choose to believe that it was an important wake-up call to prevent something even more difficult as Kim was not yet on a strong antiseizure medicine.

Our wonderful nieces were here with us, Katie from LA and Heather from Boston. They have been incredibly strong and sweet, calm and steady, so helpful and playful both. Besides bringing out wonderful humor in Kim, they spoiled me with their caring support in all ways. They've helped me realize how valuable another attentive person can be and afforded me the time to redouble my efforts to find caregiving help; we'll have someone coming in next week to start. My perseverance will pay off.

So, our days are still up and down, both in schedule as well as in Kim's energy. In a few weeks Home Health will pull away and we'll begin outpatient therapy, trading in the ease of having people come here with the benefit of a set schedule. Too, that will mark one month of our being home and a half-year since the stroke. Two seasons: a remarkable thought.

I love being home and draw sustenance from being surrounded by neighbors and friends as well as birdsong and fresh dirt. I can just step outside our front door and pull weeds anytime I want…heaven. Kim, too, is happy here in our cozy home. Just tonight he asked if I remembered having to say goodnight to him when leaving Island Rehab and how hard that was for us both. We do not lose track of how far we have both come, nor lose hope of how far we might yet go. At the same time, I realize that each moment is a gift and not to be squandered. I must remain ready to flow, to let go. It's a tribute to our growth that we stayed calm and alert, although sad, during Sunday's episode. Living so close to the edge surely helps us stay in that place of grace, gratitude, and humility.

Sending our love to you with a bow and a nod for your care.

In peace, ~ Judy

MARCH 19, 2008

Last Saturday eve was one of the most delightful and happy times I can remember. Our friend Cassie seamlessly and seemingly easily put together a dynamo concert as a fundraiser for us at an old Island hall, complete with wood floors and clear acoustics. "Gypsy Jazz" turned out to be a group with a young genius violinist, his father on guitar. Add in mandolin and percussion plus another bass guitar, and the smiles didn't quit. I'd say 100 people turned out. We've always looked to kids as barometers for "real" and so it was: The youngest set was dancing for hours nonstop, no kidding. We were surrounded by so much goodwill and kindness in friends old and new from the island and from afar. When we left at 9:00 p.m., there was much of the evening yet to go with people still trickling in. It was our first eve out since last fall and Kim held up so well; even did a few wheelin' swing steps in his chair! We did sleep well, really well, after. It was such a much-needed boost to us both. So many thanks to all who ventured out that night—to the bakers who kept everyone sweet, especially to the music groups "Ranger and the Re-Arrangers" and "Get the Oxygen Tank," and mostly to Cassie for her idea in the first place and for all of her good work joyfully given.

Last week was hard, as Kim was totally fatigued from the new meds. More like drugged, I'd say. Falling asleep during eating and therapy sessions, unresponsive so much of the time. It's been quite upsetting to me as I so need connection and communication, and too I worry that he's not eating enough because he is too tired to swallow. I've been in close contact with the neurologist and his primary doc who are tweaking the dose; this afternoon he seemed to emerge a bit more. They are willing to try another med if Kim doesn't come around by tomorrow. It's tricky alchemy.

So yes, days are full and nights are short, although we both are sleeping a bit better. I've been cheering myself up by planting flowers in the front of our home in my random-chaotic mode. There is so much sun! I feel like I'm rediscovering light. I so love the wild color and the birds that are frequenting the feeders. Really, this is a VERY cheerful home. Please join us, especially for our newest habit of afternoon tea.

I'm almost out of our old home, determined to end that chapter by this weekend. So many people have been helping out cleaning (imagine!), recycling, and sorting with me. Please do stop by to see if there is some loved treasure you can adopt. We're lightening up considerably and passing on plants, books, bowls, baskets, clothes, and household bits and pieces of all sorts to good homes. Come by this Friday evening between 5:00–6:30 p.m. or Saturday between noon and 2:00, or call for other times to take a look. After Easter, the rest will be given away. Turning the page on another chapter, and it feels just fine.

This time of intense transition too will pass. We're slowly getting into a groove of sorts, figuring out how to maneuver the chair and lift machine in the space we have, negotiating neighborhood sidewalks, learning the best curbs on which to travel, and finding a rhythm to our days. See? The difficult takes a bit of time, the impossible only a little longer. Whenever I feel frustration rise, I remember back to the not-so-distant past when I dared to wish of making a new home here, and now we are cozily settling in.

As always, I marvel at our astounding circles of support. In a curious dream last night, I was wondering why we were being given so much attention and care. I don't really need to know. I just see it, feel it, love it. Signs of you, friends and family, are everywhere: photos on the fridge, handmade blankets and paintings, homemade food, and simple gifts imbued with meaning. We continue to feel blessed and at peace and wish that for you as well, absolutely.

With much love and unabashed springtime exuberance, ~ Judy

MARCH 29, 2008

Tomorrow marks 6 weeks of being home, and tonight Kim and I were speaking of how happy we are here. This place feels like just the right size and filled with more than we need. We're comfortable and cozy; sweet Fuji seems contented too. The sun on these grey (and snowy) days finds its way in. And so many people stop by! Therapists who've been coming to work with Kim are well-humored by the flow of friends. It's a joy to be showered with such care.

I know we've been silent. Between handling daily challenges and email still not running right, we're not responding quickly to calls and letters. We bought a phone with large numbers on it so that Kim can make calls himself; you just might be the lucky recipient of one of his memorable messages. Please don't hesitate to try us too. We'll pick up if we can or we will get back to you.

I know I wrote last time about Kim's fatigue. It got to a place a few days ago where he was nearly comatose and I couldn't wake him. Another trip to the ER at Harborview, a mere 2+ weeks since the last. They kept us overnight to figure this out. The good news is that every test came back positive: no UTI, no pneumonia, vital signs strong, no other infection. Seems that what's knocking Kim out is the antiseizure med he's been on.

They sent us home yesterday with a new third med, but I cannot say I'm happy with it. At this lowest dose, he is still dopey, drugged, checked out. I miss him. These weeks have taken their toll on us as my patience wanes and frustration rises—not a good combo with the meds' impact on his moods and behavior. Not sure what the next approach will be, if another med will make a difference. It raises the critical question of safety versus quality of life, and tonight I can tell you easily where I stand.

Next week Kim will start outpatient physical therapy a block away; we have hopes that the chance to move and get a good workout will help with his strength, circulation, and spirit. He has a goal to get to a pool, which is not yet feasible as traveling in a car is still painful. Perhaps as he gets stronger, we'll be able to travel again. We do want to visit friends, to take this Camel for a l-o-n-g drive.

Music continues to be our oasis, where we go for replenishing. Singing keeps us calm during outrageous hospital dramas, connects us when we're feeling low, and gets us dancing, twirling 'round the kitchen floor when mood is right. Kim dives in when I start a song, much to my delight. Funny how such a crisis can bring us what I've long been asking for.

We're keeping perspective, grateful to be home, to have a home; happy to be alive and together. Not a given. Our community has been hit hard with critical illnesses lately. The only way I know of to weather the storms is to take slow deep breaths every day and to rest quietly in each moment—when I remember, that is. Our hearts are full, holding close to loved ones struggling for life.

With hope always, ~ Judy

April 6, 2008

I'm filling up the bird feeders daily, as these feathered fluffs are hungry for sustenance between the cold wind and rain we've been having. I love their chirping. It's a birdy place here by our "tree house."

Spring has been tough for so many. It seems to me that all the tender buds and fresh shoots that poked through a few months ago when the weather warmed so suddenly (the time Kim and I returned home) are now being hit hard by the return of the cold weather. We're tender and vulnerable, caught off-guard by the change. Dashed hopes, people letting go of life. How to hold even the weather lightly?

Our community has been stunned by loss. Once again, I am in awe of the power of living in harmony with neighbors, even if discord crops up frequently. We share grief as well as celebrations and are stronger and richer for it.

Yet here at #25 all is calm. Although we're still tweaking meds, Kim is sleeping a bit less, more like 2–3 hours a day. And when he is awake, he's incredible: interesting, funny, thoughtful, gracious, loving. I ask for no more.

Kim is still in a bit of pain, especially upon waking, but not always. I've forgotten about those months of nonstop intense migraines. I think that going to outpatient physical therapy will do wonders for his flexibility and strength (he's had one dynamo session so far). PT Martha is even daring to use the "W" word—

Walk—although I'm afraid to go there. We'll see a neuro-ophthalmologist this week to learn about his vision loss.

We've found a few good caregivers who will be able to offer me respite 3 afternoons a week. Time to head to the gym, run errands, garden, or just take a nap. This past week I managed to make it to Seattle to present on "Mediating Overseas" at a national conference with George Brose from Ohio. Last summer he retraced our journey through east Africa, meeting with those we had trained in mediation to take them to the next level; he'll return this summer. I am deeply grateful to him for his spirit and dedication to nourishing those seeds. His stories speak to how well mediation is taking root. There is no greater gift to me as a teacher than to see people running with what I've humbly offered.

We continue to be showered with visits from friends, and love it, good music and all. Truly, Kim pushes through any fog he's in when there is someone around to jolly with. I've been putting creative energy into cooking and baking, delighting when we can share food with folks dropping by.

I continue to have hope, lots of it—I just keep practicing living ever more lightly. May we all keep the sun inside and welcome the rain for deepening our faith.

With peace, ~ Judy

APRIL 17, 2008

It's been a remarkable day. Kim says I use that word too much but also agreed with me that it describes today. We went to West Sound Academy, the high school he's been teaching at, to speak with the seniors for an hour and a half. Topic? Sort of "life," our lives, about finding opportunity in crisis. Can you imagine?

I'm not sure I have words to describe how I feel. Awed at the teens' (and teachers') presence, attention, and depth of feeling. Inspired by their questions. Touched by their warmth and welcome. And totally blown away by Kim. He pulls out wisdom from a place deep inside, always coming straight from his heart. His humor weaves throughout; his spirit is strong and positive. He is unafraid, unself-conscious, open, and honest. We came home drained and contented, honored by the tenderness surrounding us. Love with a capital "L." I wouldn't have guessed that he had that kind of energy in him, but then again, he has never been predictable.

Kim is making great strides. He still sleeps during the day, but I'm beginning to think that he is adjusting to this lowest dose of meds and that this sleep is healing, for when he is awake, he's dynamo. PT Martha is working him hard and it's paying off. She is ruthless in a kind way: a strong visionary who knows what she's doing. I've learned to sit far enough away to not jump up to save him from another disastrous-looking move. And she really listens to Kim, honoring his requests and matching his witticisms. When he got off the stationary bike yesterday, he said that now he wanted to row; she thought for a moment and said "sure." Of course, I believe. She'll find a way to make it happen.

We start with an OT (occupational therapist) next week who will focus on daily living activities and, hopefully, vision. We did see a neuro-ophthalmologist last week who was decidedly unhelpful. We know that Kim sees only out of the right half of each eye and that his vision is fragmented. This doc simply said there is nothing to be done. So okay, yet another challenge to figure out. I'm asking Kim to draw or use clay to show me how he sees, for I'm guessing it's not unlike Picasso.

There is lots of hope floating around. No telling what's up next. Our days are full with therapy, docs, naps, and just managing the "ordinary" things. I'm getting in some happy gardening, putting in veggies by the house that Kim might be able to harvest. Friends continue to stop by for tea or a meal, and our kitty is thrilled for the stillness and peace. Our adventures don't take us far these days, yet there's no lack of surprise, challenge, or reward.

With thanks for you in our lives, ~ Judy

May 3, 2008

Something moved this week although I cannot name it. Everyone says that Kim looks better—more awake and alert, eyes lighter and face brighter, he is sitting straighter and sleeping less, and I noticed that somewhere in there he has stopped drooling. He says it's all being channeled into his harmonica, which perhaps is true, for he IS playing so beautifully! Really, some weight has lifted.

No doubt the sun is helping. As the weather slowly warms up, Kim is more comfortable sitting outside and soaking it in. That's got to be good for us nor'westerners. He still gets cold but at least it's now more manageable. He is eating well; I am pleased for my flexibility, cooking fish and buying meat to satisfy his carnivorous cravings. (Nothing small for a vegetarian.)

We're finding new ways to bring healing calm into our home. Music is most important. Yes, he has picked up the harmonica, inspired by our 4-year old neighbor Theo who brought over a collection of instruments when he heard us outside singing to my guitar. I cannot exaggerate how sweetly he plays and how it thrills me.

And I've had a hankering to play the folk harp, which is now becoming a reality thanks to the loan of a beautiful, hand-carved, 26-string lever harp. I hardly know how to hold it (can anyone help?), yet I am truly having fun finding melodies. It seems to be a more comforting sound than my flute as Kim drifts off to nap. And then there is aromatherapy, wonderfully calming. Smells, I believe, are a direct link to our gut.

Kim continues to work hard, doing the incredible with his PT. They are "dancing" as Kim takes steps regularly now, although still halting and painful. I'm becoming a believer. His OT is remarkable too. She has such a lovely, holistic approach, giving Kim exercises to integrate the right and left sides of his brain. It's the perfect antidote to the image of "brokenness" that started to take him over. She understands the emotions that arise, saying that sparks fly when the hemispheres communicate. Poetic and exciting, both. How lucky we are to have such tremendously caring and skilled healers in our midst.

Painful neck and leg spasms continue to plague Kim greatly, yet he is often up for making it to dinner with our community or to see a young neighbor's school play. We're getting out more. Too, we're finding support. I've started going to a support group for caregivers…we hope to, together, start going to a group for those with traumatic brain injury…and we just may start a small gathering at our home for stroke survivors.

It feels like we're in a new chapter of recovery, finding our stride and adapting to our new lives. Nights are getting a bit easier too, and for that I am extremely grateful. Our neighbors and friends, as always, add color and cheer. Blessed we are.

We do know that life is more like a feather than a rock, and so we honor each day given to us. Thank you for continuing to travel with us.

With love and good cheer, ~ Judy

MAY 11, 2008

Really, there is no reason why I should be surprised at the waves that run through our lives. I don't have to look far to understand, for all things organic have that pattern: air, water, sound. It seems that as soon as I sent off the last posting, things tilted in our little world. It's been a tough week with Kim a bit off his physical and emotional center—or maybe it was me unbalanced and he mirrored my energy. Regardless, we've made it through, and he is falling asleep in peace as I write this.

We have been tired, with neither of us sleeping well. Kim is been harboring a cold although it seems abated today. Once again, we're changing antiseizure meds, for both his therapists are convinced that the Keppra he has been on is interfering with his progress. Perhaps that's what unseated him, for he did lose his balance the other night. I hadn't paid close enough attention to notice that he had lifted up his armrest, and while I was in another room for a moment he reached over too far while doing his stretching exercises and landed with a thud on the floor. OUCH!! He is okay, he really is, with just a few small bruises. But oh! Yet another reminder of how fragile this tendril is that keeps us connected.

Describing plans at our send-off for our seven-month journey through eastern and South Africa.

There have been some wonderful high spots too. Kim made it to his first library board meeting. He was accepted to the Board last fall; this month he felt up to it and came home all excited about the committees he could join, from directing policy to aesthetics. He loves our library and has always gone there often. It's beautiful and active and within wheeling distance of our home. This has been a dream of his for a long while.

As to dreams, he speaks of an image he is holding that he wants to sculpt. Tomorrow is our day for art and music with plans to buy him his own harmonica as well as to pull out clay. I am excited to see how he responds. Kim also wants to start journaling with a tape recorder, as writing and reading remain elusive. Yay for all pathways to express. He must be carrying a pile o' stuff inside that he rarely talks about, yet the wisdom that he shares speaks to so much deep thought.

And so we manage day-to-day while holding onto the long view. I've had my first harp lesson this week and am surprisingly happy playing arpeggios and octaves. My faith in the way things work continues to strengthen me. I know we will make it, getting stronger and calmer even if it isn't in a straight line.

Thank you for witnessing our journey. Truly, that is more important than I would've imagined.

With love, ~ Judy

One day, after Kim came out with yet another story of yet another country, I demanded, "Tell me one country that you HAVEN'T been to, Kim." He thought about it for a silent minute, and then said, "Latvia, I've never been to Latvia. I was on a bus headed there once, but it broke down and so I never got to go there." After this, most of my conversations with Kim turned into me asking him just how he had managed to live such an interesting and amazing life. He never quite answered me the way I wanted him to, but I feel he'll always be a compass to me. Every time that I think of him, he's always bringing with him the gifts of quiet contemplation, a wealth of stories, and a wisdom that you have to get at yourself. His love of living has taught me countless lessons about what I want to be able to look back on myself.

Judy and Kim, you are in my daily prayers. Thank you both for being an inspiration even in a difficult time.

Be well, Sean

PART 6
EVER A TEACHER

Kim needs to be learning in order to thrive. His curiosity is never-ending. Now it's figuring out how to play the harmonica with his nondominant hand and being on the library board, something he was invited to do prestroke.

Kim is beginning to dream of reading again. He'll soon be a "consultant" with his high school. Not to mention all that he has to learn again to begin to do the daily activities we all take for granted. Kim teaches me that learning is not a luxury, it is THE reason to get up in the morning.

May 25, 2008

I've been working so hard on adapting to and accepting the "what is" of our new life that I've failed to notice all the changes happening from day to day. It's true—there are many.

Kim is so much stronger than he was even a few weeks ago. His neck is much better, probably from the terrific attention he's been getting from his chiropractor, massage therapist, and physical therapist, coupled with his sitting taller in his chair. It's making a tremendous difference, especially when riding in the van. His left leg and now his left arm are still spasming quite a bit, yet other pains seem better. His neurologist pretty much took him off of his pain meds, saying that rebound headaches happen when one takes too much of a good thing, be it narcotics or Tylenol. Even in this, Kim is amazing in that he has nearly stopped asking for them, no complaints. How adaptable he is.

Then there is Kim's therapist, Elizabeth Turner, whose specialty is with trauma. She's doing beautiful work, having him breathe space into the physical pain and diving deep into the connected emotions to move through it. How powerful it is to see Kim draw the searing red-hot pain yet with a cool blue center and soothing green around it. There is lots of hope there. Yellow fear is present too, but it is not all-consuming. And once Kim is able to release some of the pain, he draws a charred void where the pain once was. Many layers of complexity in it all. It's clear that Kim's mind is fluid and open and deeply connected to his heart. It's really exciting to watch him journey through this new territory.

As for walking, Kim is truly getting better. He still describes his stumbling steps as "baby fawn legs." Imagine him holding on to the ballet bar with all the strength he can muster, right arm shaking with tension. PT Martha is hanging onto his left side as he kicks that foot ahead, then having him make the incredibly courageous move of lifting up his right leg, trusting his standing on a leg he cannot feel. Unbelievable. I continue to hold my breath and follow too closely behind with his chair, exhausted from watching him put out the energy to hold himself up. Kim gasps, I pray silently, and his Amazonian PT is whistling "Tennessee Waltz." Quite a sight.

It's a new place for me to be the one to be cautious. I suppose that's part of the impact of this time; I've been scared. Kim is putting out his dreams to walk, to teach, to travel. I love it, support it, and also worry that he is setting himself up for goals too grand, that he'll crash when his dreams are unattainable. Yet who knows? He has already accomplished the incredible, and there is no reason to believe he won't travel much farther. I'm beginning to believe that I'm the one who is trying too hard to adapt; perhaps it's time for me to dream a little larger, too.

Summer returned today, Kim is warm (finally!), and we're taking to welcoming visitors outside. Lovely. It is fun being home, watching the daily changes in the garden outside our door. I think we both dearly miss the mountains and the sea, yet we practice focusing on all we do have. I don't think we'll ever quite be there; we just remind ourselves often. His harmonica touches a place deep inside and I love learning harp; we're forging ahead into this next chapter of our lives.

It is also a time of celebrations. So many graduates in our midst! Weddings and birthdays, too. My mother taught me to celebrate everything I can, and so we do.

Wishing us all the time to breathe deeply and bow to the richness of our lives. ~ Judy

JUNE 15, 2008

We're just back from West Sound Academy's graduation. WSA is the high school where Kim has been teaching; he is still considered staff although he hasn't been in a classroom since last September. It was an incredible, heartfelt evening. The graduating seniors are such a uniquely talented and cohesive community, and Kim was honored as well. Nellie, head of the school, acknowledged him for encouraging young people to experience the world with openness, curiosity, and a shared humanity. It's clear he has inspired many to travel and even work overseas.

Kim was the 2005 graduation speaker for his West Sound Academy students.

Also, the school's yearbook team dedicated the 2008 annual to Kim. Above a beautiful picture of him smiling warmly is written:

"Kim, your commitment to healing in the presence of your challenges is an inspiration to all of us. You lovingly touch our lives and continue to teach us today as you have in the past. Your strength gives us hope."

Graduates from past years came up to greet him, thanking him for impacting them deeply. Standing behind his chair, I am often at a great vantage point to watch faces shift as people approach. I see so much care and concern as each in turn try to understand this new version of Kim. Their tenderness touches me. And Kim somehow manages to tune in, remembering some important detail to ask about their lives. He never fails to think of others first, listening hard with his soul and his heart.

He is wanting so dearly to get back to the classroom. I know he misses the learning, the creativity, the challenge of thinking on his feet, his fellow teachers, and mostly the students. It brings out the best in him; I can envision Kim teaching in some form. In fact, he is planning on it. I worry about him setting goals that may be unattainable, yet how to discourage him at all? Who knows how far he can go? He certainly does not lack determination or desire. How hard it must be to let go of the way things were, what he so loved, and accept what is. I continue to watch with amazement, checking myself, wondering aloud, testing my assumptions. We are in a new land and there are no guidelines.

Kim so proud for WSA 2008 graduates! *The WSA 2008 yearbook dedication to Kim.*

This graduation was an important evening for me too, to remember the power of Kim before his stroke. It is hard to say aloud that I forget. I can get lost in the intensity of day-to-day existence, simply trying to maintain. I seem to be endlessly tired, surprised at how my substantial resourcefulness and creativity seem to not suffice. Life is a challenge and I bless my spirit for rising to what is asked of me, over and over yet again.

I can happily report that there hasn't been any high drama lately. We are settling into our new pace. I find that small rituals help to knit the day together, from early morning exercises through to afternoon tea and songs at evening shower time, offering some sense of stability, predictability, and comfort. Days are filled with therapies, sprinkled with wonderful visits from friends and family. Kim's sister flew out from Massachusetts and our niece from LA last weekend; his daughter and grandson will come through again next week. Nights are short, punctuated by many awakenings from the pain of his leg spasms. It's hard to understand why so far, no med has helped.

We are hoping to get out on some adventures, wanting most to breathe in the sea. We're thinking of the coast and the San Juan Islands, places close enough to get to in a few hours. We're looking for traveling companions, so please find us if you think that'd be fun! I believe Kim can now handle the jostling on major roads and the change would do us both good.

Slowly, slowly we inch forward, never daring to let go of hope. It's a fine balance: holding acceptance on one end, actively pursuing change on the other. My definition of "balance" is no longer walking the tightrope, but of "waddling"—for leaning too far in one direction is balanced out by leaning too far in the other.

Thinking of you all, feeling surrounded by your tremendous circle of care.

With love, ~ Judy

July 7, 2008

I had a feeling that I was pressing my luck when I wrote in the last update that there hadn't been any "high drama" lately. The next morning Kim had a seizure. His second and a minor one, yet the aftermath so ramped up his vital signs that I called our friends at 911. A week later, there was yet another. The only lasting (observable) impact is that the dose of his antiseizure medicine has been increased. His heart continues to be strong and steady and his blood pressure remains low, although he is back to sleeping 4 to 5 hours during the day most likely because he is still not sleeping much at night. Ah, so it goes.

Days fly by, weeks too. Our desire to travel is on pause for now as it is hard to work around Kim's energy. Whatever oomph he does have goes to physical therapy, where he pushes himself so hard to learn to walk again. He continues to teach me about the simple pleasures and so we do—fresh eggs for breakfast, smells of breads and cookies baking, growing veggies, taking in the flowers, listening deeply to music, loving the birds (cedar waxwings this week!), soaking up the sun, and having a purring kitty by our side. Too, the warmth in the air has lured Kim outdoors; he has been comfortable for the first time in months. It's a quiet, calm, and peaceful life and yes, very different from what we lived before.

Changes are slower in coming, though I do believe we're still on the upward trajectory. Just this past week we went to another eye doc who is trying Kim out on reading glasses with prisms to help clear up his distorted vision. It just may help, and it has given us hope that he will be able to read again…

…which will come in handy even more so this fall, when Kim returns to West Sound Academy! It's true, though not in the teaching capacity he's been used to. Kim has been offered the position of "Consultant" for the upper-school humanities teachers. It sounds incredibly wonderful for him. He has been told that the school especially needs his global awareness and human rights perspective. Best, is that he won't have to grade papers. Perfect. Just to add to the surprise, I've been asked to work with the middle-schoolers in a sort of counselor position. All of it is still very sketchy, yet this tendril connecting us to West Sound is quite a gift.

We've now passed through 3 seasons since Kim's stroke. We've been at home as long as we've been in hospitals and rehab centers. It is still a bit much for me to fully comprehend. I do best when I stay in the present and flex with what is in front of me; letting go of expectations remains my constant challenge. Your unbelievable support and attention help us both adapt to what has been given to us.

We thank you, always, for being nearby. We send blessings your way.

Love, ~ Judy

JULY 30, 2008

Midsummer is an exquisite time of year! We're happy at home, soaking up sun and feasting eyes and bellies on our garden. The air is sweetened by lavender and jasmine; the flowers continue to surprise. Today we ate our first cucumber, the peas are about done, and our lettuce has fed us as well as in many a community meal. Our tomatoes are a whopping 5' tall, and the pole beans are wrapping around everything they can find. We did harvest a stunning purple cauliflower the size of a basketball and sweet throughout. Starting to put in a fall and winter garden, a new venture for me. Birds seem to feel comfortable here too, as our sweet kitty Fuji ignores them. My hammock is now up and terribly inviting; I could easily flitter away hours watching the birds chatter away as they feast.

Kim seems to be exceptionally tired today. Eating has been tougher for him and his balance is a bit off. Could be that he isn't sleeping well, could be just a phase, could be me projecting my weariness onto him. It doesn't matter; I only appreciate each day that much more. I know that he is always doing the best he can, stretching himself in more ways than I'll ever comprehend. I am a witness to his daily rallying, here to tell you that Kim is astounding in his courage, perseverance, and strength.

We've had a few bumps in the road, though nothing that has stopped Kim from continuing to work hard at walking. Twice a week his PT gets him standing, learning how to move—and trust—his left leg. I know it's the most important part of the week for him and the only time he warms up from the inside out. I so hope that someday he'll again have the feeling of moving on his own. It is powerful to watch him coordinate all 6'3". I so love to see the full length of his body stretch tall.

We're still waiting for his trifocal prism "John Lennon" glasses to be done. Could be tomorrow. Could be revolutionary. There is hope that these will help

Kim figure out the images of his world, making it easier for him to travel in the van as well as focus in on faces. He is well aware that it's hard for others when he doesn't make eye contact, yet now it's too difficult for him to see features. He describes us all as cubist images á la Picasso.

With his temporary reading glasses, Kim can read. He sat at the computer today for a bit, though he gets headaches too easily. He is lost in imagination a lot these days, no doubt making up for his inability to read others' ideas. I so wish he'd start writing again. Friends are making it possible for us to try out a voice-activated computer software program that we'll purchase soon. Stay tuned.

So the weeks pass. We're nestled at home while friends and neighbors take off on long trips to all corners of the world. I'm aware of how my sense of time is changing; days bob up and down rather than follow each other in a line. Time is cyclical yet somewhat suspended. I'm no longer in a hurry to go anywhere or get anything done, incredible as that is to say aloud. Rather, we pay attention to how we are with each other and in community, knowing beyond all doubt that relationships are the cornerstone of our lives. When I told Kim that I was about to write another update, he said, "Tell them of our love." Yes, it's as strong as ever.

We hope that your summer, too, is peaceful and fruitful. It is a treat to hear of your adventures; we welcome stories, always. May we stretch these beautiful days and appreciate the warmth and bounty of this season.

With love and care, ~ Judy

August 23, 2008

It's been a full yet rocky month since I last wrote; I'll do my best to capture the highlights. I can say that today, the river we're in is once again flowing smoothly and I am breathing easily once more.

YES to Kim's John Lennon glasses working! And how distinguished he looks. These trifocal prisms seem to bring a fragmented world into focus and Kim is able to read. It's slow going, though, and results in headaches, for the processing of what he sees demands a lot of his brain. Kim wore them for over 2 hours today—a new record. Although he is not prone to gushing, I think he's mighty pleased. We owe a lot to our eye doc who figured this one out.

In an effort to end the ongoing saga of leg spasms, we will see "Dr. Botox" next week to give injections a try. The idea is that Botox will relax Kim's tense muscles enough to reduce the spasms. He has also been experiencing being zapped by electricity, sometimes for an hour or more. It looks quite painful. Seizures have been coming around every 4 weeks or so. Yet there is so much we and docs don't know, including if these seizures are perhaps intense full-body spasms or even minor strokes.

And just to thicken the plot, Kim's swallowing has gotten progressively worse over the last 4 weeks to the point where he is been unable to eat much at all. There is no way for me to describe the anguish of watching him stare at a plate of food knowing that he'll most likely end up coughing. Forget the pleasure of taking big bites. He has been eating so very s-l-o-w-l-y and mindfully, no talking allowed. Where he used to eat 2–3 pancakes with gusto, last week he was doing his best to down a small one in 1+ hours. We've been doing smoothies daily and blenderizing everything. It's still not working, and I've been plagued with nightmares of him starving. My alarms to docs finally worked and yesterday we saw our neurologist. They gave Kim a barium swallow test. Turns out that this could be all due to acid reflux; he is on a med that might take care of it. Please, may it truly be this easy an answer.

So much for the medical side of life. Our dance card continues to be astoundingly packed with visits from the best of folks. We have wonderful friends and tremendous support from family as well. Our bro-in-law just left today after nearly a week of helping out; my 85-year-old relatives will show up next weekend, driving from northern CA. Some pretty neat networking tends to happen in our little home too, as friends meet friends and find they have so much in common!

Kim's spirit remains remarkably strong and loving throughout. We are both sleeping better too; the difference it makes for me is tangible. I am slowing letting go of the old Kim and the life we had created, beginning to appreciate this new place we're in. I can honestly say that our summer has been good: warm sun, bountiful garden, and the music of birds. It's a treat to be home and see patterns in how days unfold. We keep creating new rituals, finding ways to structure our days and celebrate life. We love playing with language: Kim feeds me a "word challenge" each morning; we've begun to read (and memorize) poetry and spent a week speaking French with our neighbor's beautiful French granddaughters. It's surprisingly satisfying to be right here, not expecting much doing.

Our focus is pretty close to home these days, which is not the usual for either of us. We do take in what is happening in the world; perhaps more immediate is what is happening in our little community—a microcosm. I marvel at how we take care of each other as teens leave for college, neighbors struggle through surgery and illness, and babies are welcomed into the world. We remain grateful for the gift each of you brings and thank you deeply for your care and company.

Wishing peace to us all as summer fades into autumn, ~ Judy

September 10, 2008

I had a dream a few nights ago that I was returning sea creatures to the water. The tide was out and I was concerned that they couldn't wait, so I got a hose and started filling in the tide. I quickly realized how futile that was! Besides, I knew the water would come in on its own, in its own time. But by the time I put down the hose, my bucket of creatures had been pulled out to sea; they were moored at a rock too far out for me to swim to. I had to trust that the bucket would turn over and they would be released. I had to let go.

We've been in a deep trough this month. Kim's swallowing is getting worse, in spite of the change in meds and the "good swallow" report a few weeks ago. I've been emailing and calling the docs. More appointments are coming up, yet no one knows what is going on. Kim is growing weaker and hungrier, now being sustained largely by Ensure with a few mashed bites of real food. Meals are no longer relaxing social times and we miss eating with the community. We may soon be facing the decision of putting in a feeding tube again. I must trust that the tide will come in soon, and in time.

Yet through it all (I hope this isn't a boring refrain), Kim remains my inspiration, my light. He somehow finds a way to enjoy blenderized soup, doesn't complain at not being able to eat what he wants, and hasn't mentioned beer and chips for over a year. I don't sense any anger, rather extreme frustration and deep sadness. He is extraordinary in every way, gracious with everyone, loving throughout.

Kim did turn older yesterday—his 68th. We had a simple dinner with a few friends, then invited the community over to share an ice cream cake (is there any other kind?). It was wild in here for a brief half hour (standing room only), filled with joyful energy and good wishes.

So please keep us in your thoughts and hearts. I'm doing everything I can think up to help Kim heal, and canceling what I can to preserve the bit of energy Kim does scrape together. I trust you will understand when we don't return calls or emails promptly; we hope to again soon and we certainly think of you, dear friends and family.

I recently came across the simple reminder that in the end, what matters most is how well we lived, how well we loved, and how well we learned to let go. Maybe this is our time to practice.

Blessings and love to all, ~ Judy

After a Painting by Edward Hopper

by Kim Bush

*On the gray cold evening
I'm dazzled by you,
Hopper.*

*Soaked with sun
she sits,
Surrounded by
      whiteness
           that should glare
yet only heats.*

*It's not stark
    or drab,*

*But white—a pure, hot
    white that
        heats me
on this gray cold evening.*

September 28, 2008

Kim woke up this morning dreaming of barbecued Ensure. I'm not clear if he meant in the container or not, but you get the idea. He is thinking about food much of the time; it's become our life. Ensure scrambled eggs, Ensure pudding, and his favorite: Ensure smoothies (read: "ice cream"). My creativity has found a niche.

    He IS better. His energy is stronger and we're both adjusting to a new normal. Truly, it is amazing to me how we humans adapt. Kim still takes most of the day to eat. Meals still run 1–2 hours, and he still cannot swallow anything that doesn't melt in his mouth. Yet that is okay—for he seems to be getting enough nourishment to maintain. Our expectations of a day have flexed. Neither of us spends much time lost in regret or sentimentality.

Kim told me his mother's description of his first day in first grade, and how Kim let go of her hand and walked surely and eagerly to school, never looking back. I love this quality in him, this boundless curiosity and adventurous spirit drawn to the unknown. His quest for learning and growing never lets up. Reason enough to get up in the morning.

This week we passed the anniversary of Kim's stroke. The first day of autumn dawned as crisp and sunny as it did last year; it wasn't much of a stretch to remember that day's events. We invited for tea the couple who had come upon us on the trail and dropped into our story: angels, surely. We never learned their names then; they walked through our community a month ago and found us. We spent a delightful afternoon getting to know them, recounting blessings and talking of how we each choose to live.

We still have no answers about what is going on with Kim's swallowing in spite of the many tests he's been through; more are slated. We're looking at all possibilities, from hormone levels to helping his body release the tension from past traumas. We're flowing with it as we can, neither holding our breaths nor expecting miracles. Kim knows that he may be faced with some tough decisions soon if his swallowing keeps getting weaker.

This closeness to the edge only creates in us the desire to live more fully, only increases our gratitude. We laugh more easily and live slowly, quietly. A wise friend, sculptor Tom Jay, once said, "You can't go deep if you don't go slow."

Many of you contacted us after my last update. Beautiful words and messages. Thank you so much for your concern and your care. I cannot exaggerate how important your connection is for us especially now, as we are limiting visits to match Kim's energy. Yet please do feel free to call or stop by as you are so moved; I am pretty good at being honest about timing. We welcome your reaching out.

As the weather begins to close in around us, may we all keep the sun and warmth inside. Snuggling season. Colors are rich, and the air has that freshness to it that thrills me. We're still reaping bounty from our little garden. It's a good time of year for homing in on what is most important and for dreaming. We're doing both. And I'm slowly beginning to understand how it is that our friends in Africa, living with so little buffer, have such a tremendous capacity for joy. Ah, yes!

In peace, ~ Judy

November 3, 2008

Life has been, happily, undramatic. We've hit a sort of stride. Days dissolve easily into one another; weeks roll on by. We have figured many things out and have created all sorts of rituals—some for efficiency, many for fun. Patterns and some sense of predictability are comforting.

Trees have turned from green to gold and flaming red, and now leaves are nearly fallen. I'm hard-pressed to know exactly when that happened, although I am watching closely. I can still pull robust carrots and potatoes out of the ground and we're eating the last of the cucumbers; plenty of kale and lettuce are left for sharing. Not sure if the rest of the tomatoes will ripen. And the apples, exceptional! It's been a beautiful autumn.

I'm fascinated with how time has become cyclical. For once I'm off of the "conveyor belt" that has a beginning and an end. We're not going anywhere, not striving to reach a destination. Our focus, if any, is on deepening our moments together and with others. I'm that much more of a human being rather than a human doing and am surprisingly at peace with that.

I don't think much has changed this past month. Kim's ability to swallow has not improved, yet we expect nothing more. No new answers. Kim chose to cancel the few dates he had with specialists, explaining that he is content with what is. Meals of a soft-boiled egg or a cup of soup still take 1–2 hours. The flavors of Ensure please him and his love of mixing things up means that we always have new (unrepeatable) combos of tastes, i.e., potato soup with squash with mashed-up something. Our friend and neighbor Molly gifted us with a hand-blender that can turn any food into mush—just perfect.

Kim has days where he is quite tired and needs to sleep, and others where he surprises me with his tenacity and attention. He still has a lot of pain in his head, neck, and left side, although he carries it without complaint. He still has seizures (another one this eve). I wouldn't say that I see much progress in his brave attempts to walk, though his story will be different. Yet no more back pain, for the new mattress we got him is working wonders.

His humor is as irreverent as ever (he gets away with a lot); he somehow manages to draw a smile out of everyone. Kim's will is strong too, which can be pretty interesting as it can be a challenge to try and reason with him. A good sign, I say, for it is all too clear to me how vulnerable he must feel. I wish him any sense of control possible, so I stretch yet more and end up learning anew.

Today we joined the Unitarian Universalist Church. (Jewish Buddhists are welcomed!) It's a warm-hearted congregation and we're drawn especially to the social justice work. The new husband-wife minister team is full of music, drama, and play; many of our friends and neighbors attend as well. We find it inspiring and grounding both, always offering food-for-thought. Today's sermon was on grief and loss, especially timely as our cohousing community lost yet another neighbor a week ago (a courageous and lovely 17-year-old succumbed to cancer). No chance to deny death; we find more solace by diving in and talking about it. There was an altar upon which we could place a photo of someone who had died. Kim chose to put a picture of his "old" self; I found one of him rowing his peapod looking so happy, so strong. Beautiful. We both grieve the loss of that Kim while getting to know and love this new one. I am pleased that they have a lot in common.

Although the weather has turned and Kim is wearing yet more layers of clothes in an effort to keep warm, we're managing to get out a bit for other than therapies and doctors. An evening of music here, a movie there, some community volunteering, engagement in cohousing activities, and life feels full and plenty rich. You, friends and family, remain incredibly supportive and caring, absolutely the cornerstone of our lives. We feel mighty blessed.

So yes, we are happy. I am learning to live with keen, watchful attention while breathing deeply, knowing that this river is always changing. "Stay bent" is how we used to take leave from friends in my Forest Service days in Idaho decades ago; only now does it truly make sense.

With love and peace in my heart, ~ Judy

No Regrets

~ In Memory of Kim Bush ~

by Lydia Harvey, 2010 WSA graduate

How has a person lived so well
That they may pass without regret?
It is a teacher's imparted wisdom
That leads to works of wonder.
So many priceless memories
Shared with the future.

How wonderful is the gift you gave
Of a life filled with kindness.
Dedicated to learning and teaching alike,
It is an inspiration to generations
With strength of self through the hardest times.

All good teachers leave a special something,
A certain unique mark upon the world
Giving students something to live by
Because the world is not nearly enough.

Search farther than the moon, you told us.
Reach higher than the stars, you said.
Never sway in your beliefs and live without regret.

This lesson we will hold
And this wisdom we will impart.
So that someday, we too,
May, without regret, depart.

PART 7
THE COMFORT OF RITUALS

One year in. How far we've come, how surprised we are by both the challenges and the blessings. I have zero time to imagine anything different, and so—our feet held to the fire—we make it through each day. I can report that it takes two hours to get Kim up every morning and three hours at night from the time he says he's ready to sleep until he is in bed.

We find that daily rituals give us handrails in an uncertain time, a sense of structure as well as meaning. Time stretches, it morphs, it stands still, it limps. And rituals help to hold it in place.

NOVEMBER 26, 2008

Replenish. That's our word, our hope for the week. We're both quite weary and stretched thin. Kim had 3 seizures in the last 3 weeks, and Sunday's was weird enough (complete with head twitching, eyes rolling back, and rapid blinking) that the doc-on-call urged us to make haste to the ER. Nothing showed up, all tests normal. Just tired, for Kim was exhausted from the exertion and I am calm but with antennae on full alert 'round the clock.

This month has also been one of grappling with many decisions from dealing with a dying stereo system and a dead printer to a change in health insurance for both of us. Too, I've been crazed by the pharmaceutical industry, finding such wild discrepancies that I'm outraged and scrappy. We've also had a small crisis with our superb caregiver that left us without any help for too long; hopefully we've resolved that one. It's been a harsh lesson in how vulnerable we are. Add to that the exciting outcome of the election and the economic climate we're in, and voilà, a month as dramatic as the weather!

The cream of this cookie-of-a-month was a weekend with family from both coasts: Kim's sister Susie and niece Heather with her 18-month-old daughter Esme, all from

MA, and niece Kate with husband Doug from LA. The 7 of us snuggled easily into this tree house of a cozy home, happily entertained by little Esme who brought out the goofy in each of us. Our early Thanksgiving was delightful and delicious.

One of the outcomes of that weekend was the discovery of pumpkin cheesecake. Really, Kim and I have mastered the cuisine of high-fat soft foods. Tonight's feast for Kim was mashed chicken tortellini alongside scalloped oysters, pumpkin cheesecake with cranberry sauce, and dulce-de-leche ice cream for dessert. (Fellow vegetarians take note of where love can lead!) Kim has been known to purr. I am happy to report that he has not lost any more weight in the last few months.

Besides thinking up new treats, we've been having fun with our community, organizing a "Winter Wanderlust" series of armchair traveling…to pulling off a quick recycling skit with kids…to opening our home to a "Grief Circle" for quiet conversation.

We also pulled off the incredible and made it to Dr. Parke's early-morning, 10th-grade ethics class at West Sound Academy a few weeks back. We talked to the students about the "compass" we use to make decisions in life and how we find happiness. It was a stunning morning for us, for the students' attention was incredible, their stories powerful, and their letters to us deeply touching.

So, as we head into the season of giving thanks, we think of you. It's your love and support that help us get through the troughs and companion us as we ride the crests. We thank you truly and wish us all the moments of nurture and rest that replenish.

With gratitude, ~ Judy

December 21, 2008

Once again I'm struck by the power we have in choosing the stories we create about our lives.

A week ago, Kim and I were sitting in the University of Washington Medical Center eating lunch while waiting for our appointment with Dr. Botox. Without warning, Kim burst into tears. My heart broke. When I could understand what grieved him so, he said that he had stepped outside the scene and was watching us, me feeding him yogurt and with a plastic spoon at that. He felt so sad that I was "stuck" with him. Painful image. After some silence, I said that perhaps another way to see us was to look not at what we were doing as much as how we were with each other—tender, loving, kind, playful. Feeding someone is an act of devotion, of nurture. He calmed quickly.

Later that night we dove into the difference between "pathetic" and "loving." How we can focus past what first meets the eye and read what gentleness, patience, and faces reveal. We can choose what we see; it's a happier way to live.

Yet it's been a time of major disappointment for Kim. He saw an orthopedic doc this week for the pain in his knees, one he had been to over 3 years ago. The good news is that his arthritis hasn't gotten worse and he doesn't need surgery; the harder news is that the doc told Kim that it doesn't look like he'll walk, at least not in the near future. It's not news to me, who has been watching him like a mother hawk for months, but it is for Kim! In spite of the odds, he has held onto a vision of getting on his bike again, hopping (his word) into his boat, hiking, and more. It appears that he's not heard anyone's voice but that of his Amazonian PT, who has been leading him on for months. I'm deeply sad for Kim and furious at the setup.

I'm not sure of the aftermath of this news. Kim's been sleeping a lot, has had low energy. Could be the cold (and beautifully white) weather, could be this season of darkness and dreaming. I think he is working hard on creating a different story to understand this new world he's in. Yet he rallies for visitors as always and has spurts of excitement, especially when talking to his daughter and grandson. He is ever the learner and has been wanting to learn Portuguese, and so we've started.

In spite of his disappointments, Kim's humor is ever-present. We laugh often and heartily. Here is a smattering of the many names he calls our sweet (13-year-old) kitty Fuji: Jingles…Gretchen…Triscuit…Fluff-Bottom…Dixie…Squeaky…Wrinkles…Crinkles…Binky…Daphne…Miss Fancy-Pants…Spunky…and Giggles, my favorite.

We continue to be gifted by neighbors, friends, and family, waking up to presents almost daily. Today it was a few more 6-packs of Ensure left by our thoughtful neighbor, Michiko, in case I can't get to the store in the carpet of snow that fell last night. Sharon brought us a white rose yesterday; Missi left beautiful pears in our new vestibule. And Kim's oldest friends from Brown U days (we're talking 50 years of friendship), Andy and Susan, stunned us with an exquisite Bose radio/CD that brings hours of comfort and joy. Aye, we're well cared for.

So please don't feel sorry for us. We don't. We're living out the lives we've been given, best we can. Yes, my heart breaks as Kim's must, too. Yet I don't believe that any of us merits grace more than another. Fate has a way of handing us what we need in order to become whole, and in a surprising way, I think we are. Perhaps it takes being broken before we can heal. I don't know. What I do know is that I could not have imagined a love this profound and expansive. Bernie sent us a card that quotes Lao Tzu: "To love someone deeply gives you strength. Being loved by someone deeply gives you courage." Our lives are infinitely rich.

So here is a toast to us all as we enter the heart of the winter, the solstice, and this season of celebration. We'll be hunkered down at home, ready with hot tea and treats if you'd care to come by and share stories and cheer. The days are turning, once again beginning the long journey toward light. May we continue to find gratitude in the small things each day and gain strength from our connections to each other. We're thinking of you with open hearts and so much love.

Blessings and peace, ~ Judy

P.S. In case you're wondering, Kim's Botox treatment is not for ridding wrinkles but for reducing spasms! Let's hope it works.

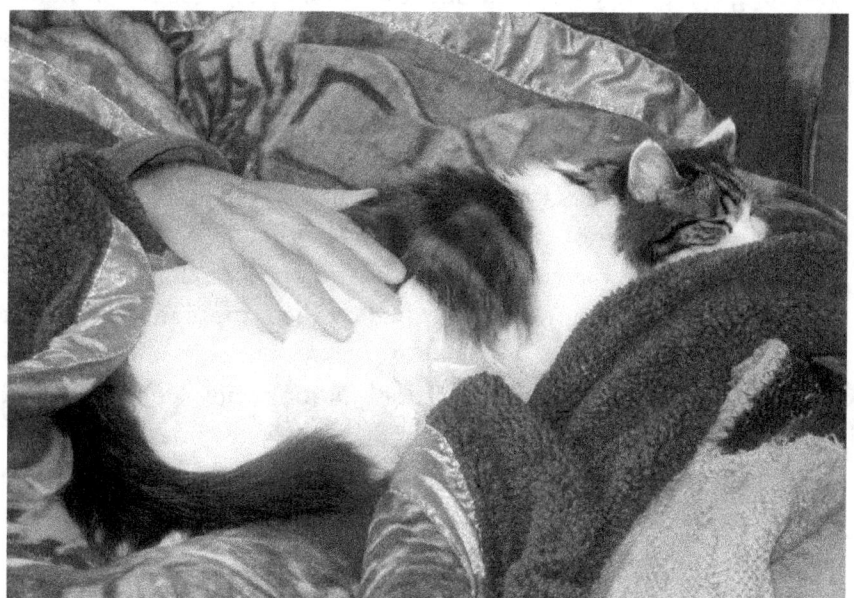

Kitty Fuji doing her job, holding Kim down during his long daily naps.

January 19, 2009

What a remarkable start to the new year! And what a change from my last update. (Seems to be the nature of life and living, these undulating waves.) Picture Kim in his wheelchair propelling himself with both of his feet. He is now able to lift up his left leg, move it forward, and put it down. Albeit slowly, but my word! He says it's a feeling of freedom. It's honestly miraculous to watch. I can only imagine that his leg is relearning the pattern from the time he's been putting in on a rehab bike with his new PT.

Yup, we've switched physical therapists, and Keith is a wonder. Calm, intensely thoughtful, intuitive, and wise, he listens so well to Kim's body and is creating an innovative path for Kim to strengthen and heal. He is not ruling out walking, just knows that there are some things that have to come first, like knowing where that errant left leg is in space. I no longer hear Kim bemoan not walking; rather, he is mighty excited about biking and what we're calling "cake walking." Too, he actually warms up and at times sweats—a great relief. Hallelujah! Just to add to the delight, this new PT setting has huge windows that let in the southern light and classical music to calm the restless. Downstairs is a sweet-smelling flower shop with an espresso café. Ah, so many reasons to drop by and work out.

On Tuesday, we'll head to a new speech therapist to check for any insights into Kim's thinning voice and continued difficulty swallowing. He is also wanting to work on reading and possibly writing, two activities that still elude him. Neither of us are expecting wonders; it just feels like a good time to try again.

I think Kim is getting a lot of energy from returning to the teacher/mentor role. Thanks to the hearts and creative thinkers at West Sound Academy, the senior class is coming to our home to talk about what they're studying in their humanities classes—a pair of students each week. They bring such vitality! Kim loves it, looks forward to the visits, and has me doing research on the web and in the library just because. I am deeply touched by the respect and graciousness of these young adults.

Kim has been holding steady. No seizures, nothing unusual. We've carved out a daily pattern that feels doable: mornings at therapies, teatime with visitors. His sleep is erratic at night, better during the day during his usual 2-hour afternoon nap. Our sweet kitty has taken her accompanying job seriously and holds him down for the full snooze.

We're having fun learning Portuguese; it stretches our brains and Kim is a quick study (make this language #6 for him). I, as well as others, have been reading aloud all sorts of books. The latest was *The Education of Little Tree*, a gem of a story that seems to have triggered many dreams of his dad, grandfather, and grandson. And we continue to be as involved with our community as energy allows. Ma Nature is revving up too. Bulbs are beginning to show their green shoots; I can feel my fingers getting itchy for soil. Days are lengthening and when the sun comes out, I am giddy with energy.

In a mere two days, Obama will be President. Imagine! He has already given us the gift of hope and continues to awe me with his vision and willingness to listen. We need his courage, strength, centeredness, leadership, and spirit. The only way I know to take in the news around the globe, is to act. I carry these words of Diane Ackerman: "I swear I will not dishonor my soul with hatred, but offer myself humbly as a guardian of nature, as a healer of misery, as a messenger of wonder, as an architect of peace." May I live into them.

So there you have it. In less than a month, we'll mark a full year, four seasons, of being home. Unbelievable. Back to gratitude once again, for there is no way we could have gotten here without all of the care, support, and help from you, our loving family and friends.

Blessings to all, ~ Judy

February 13, 2009

Kim loves to laugh. If I start chuckling at how he purrs when he eats (which he is doing now more than ever), his dimples start to show and a smile comes across his face. It's contagious. I'm finding that even I'm waking with a happy heart, something Kim has always done though I cannot say the same for me. Playing is not just for puppies.

We're happy together, perhaps more than ever. We're a strong team as long as we focus on what we can do, not on what we can do no longer—and I'm getting there. We really can do a lot. Kim's strength is with people, creating a safe and welcoming, nonjudgmental, gracious space. Teens respond, and now we've been asked to work with kindergarteners who are studying peacemakers, as well as third-graders in disability awareness. What a treat! We're still doing Diversion with teens and parents (a restorative-justice approach for youth charged with misdemeanors), and his West Sound students add immeasurably to our days. Kim has also been talking of working with vets coming home from Iraq, for he too understands something of trauma. Please don't let us forget all of you who bring endless presents of energy, food, and food-for-thought. My greatest challenge is just in stretching our days.

I certainly notice Kim's improvement overall. His stamina is better, he's tracking better, and his humor never ceases to amaze me. His biking is paying off, for now he can move his left leg and arm higher still. I see his joy in his progress and am thrilled along with him.

For those of you concerned about me, I thank you for your care. You're right—I don't write these updates when I'm having the fall-aparts or when I'm exhausted. Yet I really feel like I know about listening to my body (except for a cold, neither of us has been sick for 2 years) and doing the best I can to get to the gym, eat healthy, and take time to play.

Yet I've had another lesson in empathy and humility this week as well as a major wake-up call for me, for us. I was struck with a TIA on Tuesday, a ministroke that didn't last long, yet made a lasting impression. I remember it vividly, as I was quite curious and working hard to figure things out: "Ah, this too." Paralysis on my right side…not able to move…doing repetitive motions…not able to speak and then when I could, unable to find words. It was Kim who helped me decipher what hit me, though you'd think I was versed in these warning signs. And it was his genius to have me find words in Portuguese, of all things, when English eluded me (and it worked!). Thanks to friends and our wonderful caregiver Alicia who made it through heavy snow to get to us so that I could get to the ER. (How utterly odd to be the one on the gurney.)

Our doc said that I have none of the risk factors for this TIA, that stress wouldn't cause this. Still, we've been planning to have Alicia come and help us for a full day a week, and I continue to look for more support as well. On Valentine's Day, we have a few friends who live on the Island coming over to be trained in an emergency—a very heartfelt gift. My only request is to please trust that I'm doing everything I can think up, taking in ideas, and making thoughtful decisions. We keep tweaking to make our lives work.

Yet I can truly say that our days are happy and our gratitude is genuine. I'm hardly just caregiving. I love this man. My sister got it right: We can do this because of the love we share. We have incredible conversations, sacred times, and new dreams to follow. Kim remains the best of companions and takes care of me as well, though in perhaps different, all-important ways.

It is nearly Valentine's Day. May we all find love that gives us such strength and courage, for I'm convinced that that is what makes our world go 'round.

With love from us both, ~ Judy

March 30, 2009

It's peaceful in this home this afternoon. Fuji is curled up on the couch (she never seems to lose her appetite for sleep), I'm dreaming of taking a nap, and Kim is quietly reading the paper.

Wait a minute. Did you catch that? Kim is reading the paper! *The New York Times* to be exact. On a Kindle—an e-reader that can download just about any book, magazine, or newspaper instantly. It looks like a grown-up iPod with a font large enough that Kim can read and a small-enough screen that he can scan to the left and not get confused by too much on a page. This is a dream come true, a gift from our techno-age. This morning he wanted to hear the "thud" of the newspaper being delivered and so I obliged, though it's of course downloaded silently and long before he awakens.

He has just started a book: Richard Bode's *Beachcombing at Miramar* that takes us to the water, one of our favorite places. We've been on a jag reading Bode, loving his descriptions of "climbing the wind" as he sails the Great South Bay near where Kim grew up. I cannot put into words what it does to me to hear Kim read aloud. I am endeared to his halting, raspy voice and the tenderness behind it.

Kim's reading is helped by the eye exercises he began last week. It's a home vision therapy program that works on our computer and gets sent back to the eye doc who tracks his progress. The exercises are helping him scan to the left as well as coordinate his eyes so that they work together better. It's not easy stuff (quite exhausting actually), and yet Kim has tremendous energy and perseverance.

We've been holding steady and then some. No new episodes; physical therapy is continuing beautifully—Kim is getting closer to standing near 6'3" on his own. We're sleeping well enough, staying healthy. Kim's left leg is getting stronger, the right one is holding up well, and overall, he is moving much more fluidly.

Our exceptional caregiver, Alicia.

Too, I've been training our terrific caregiver, Alicia, to get Kim up in the morning. At the end of the month I will take advantage of this and spend the day flying to San Francisco to see my sister, our first visit in 2 years. Between Alicia and our bro-in-law Kevin who's coming out from MA, Kim will be in good hands. This is the first time Kim and I will be apart for more than a few hours since September 2007.

A class of third-graders fed our hearts this week. Imagine twenty-plus kids sitting on a rug around Kim, looking up at him with wide-eyed patience and curiosity. Kim connected immediately by asking if he reminded them of their grandfather. Hands shot up: "Your white hair!" "Your mustache!" "Your smile!" Kim spoke of the changes in his life, answered questions about paralysis, showed off his "cake walk," and found humor in it all. The kids were captivated and so respectful. Here are some of the heartfelt excerpts from the thank-you letters we just received (spelling left unchanged):

- *I know what it's like to have disiblities a tiny bit now.*
- *Thank you for teaching us about disabilities it was very interesting and it really changed the way I looked at disabled people it really helped me almost feel what it feels like to be disabled, it was really helpful to me. Thank you so much.*
- *I know you don't know how to read but I hope you like my card. I think you and Judy are a grat cuple.*
- *I learned a lot from you yesterday. YOU ROCK!! It was amazing that you could move your paralyzed left arm and leg!*
- *I thought it was vary speshl of you to come to are class room. I hope Kim well be able to complete his goels of walking and standing up by hiss self...for if you can ackomplish your goels, then any budy can do it to.*
- *I thought a paralyzed person couldn't move at all, but I was wrong. You can move really good. Really, really good.*
- *Your visit to the classroom has so far been my favorite in the three to four years I've been in school.*

Our days have a reassuring pattern. We get up two hours before we need to leave for therapy or a doc...return home for a late lunch...catnap for an hour or two...then often have tea with friends before dinner. It still takes Kim hours to eat; 5 hours or more a day are spent in mindful chewing. Add in biking and eye exercises and perhaps you can forgive us if our "dance card" seems unusually full. The routine is spiced up with student visits and friends. Since I last wrote, we spent memorable time with Ohio friends Julie and Lowell, who taught alongside Kim in Ecuador in the 1970s, as well as with one of my oldest friends, Jeanette, my most favorite flute duet partner from Idaho days in the 1980s. How lucky we are.

It is now officially spring—birds are slowly beginning to return to our bird feeders and I've just ordered a solar birdbath so that I can be a shameless voyeur. Flowers are brilliant; hyacinths sweeten the air. Lettuce and spinach are slowly poking through the still-cold soil, though I think the peas may need to be replanted. And the tips of the maple branches outside our bedroom window are showing red. We've made it through a long winter unscathed. Yet many we know have not been so lucky. Kim's Aunt Luffy closed her eyes for the last time on the first day of spring, age 97. A close friend has been diagnosed with cancer. And another in Burundi just lost his wife and third child in childbirth. Our hearts are with these families. The seasons keep turning as do our lives, and times are not always kind.

May we all draw strength from the energy of the earth, the power of the sun, the clarity in the wind, the hope of the stars, and the comfort of the moon.

Thank you for your love and care. ~ Judy

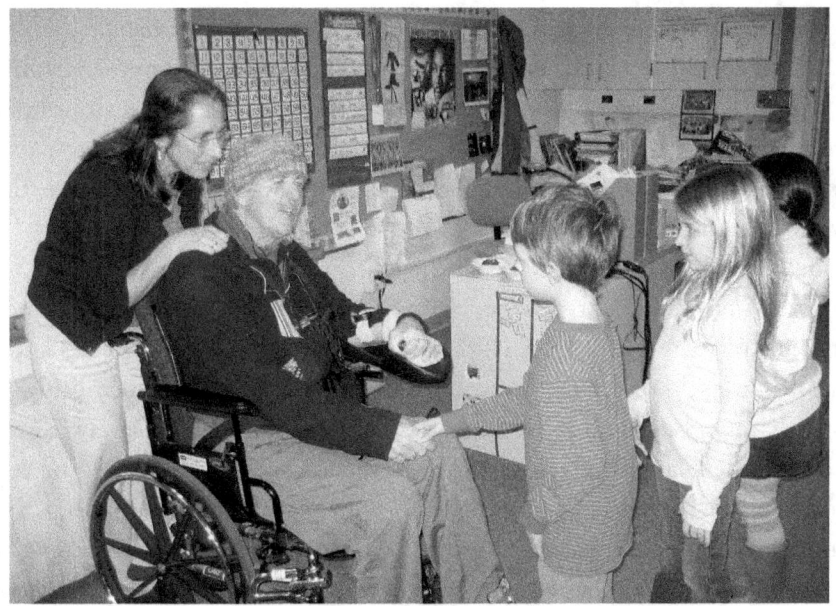

Kim shaking every student's hand at the end of a disability awareness program for third-graders—so much respect both ways.

MAY 20, 2009

We're coming on two months since I've last written. A lot has gone on, yet there is a familiar regularity in our days. "Routine" or "ritual?" I find this a fascinating contrast, one that can make the difference between a life that's full and rich…or a life one endures…though nothing may appear different from the outside looking in. It is a choice.

Yes, ritual. Our days are filled with them, from the morning's "greet the day" practice and our daily stop at the "kissing station" on the way from the bathroom to the kitchen…all the way to the end of the day and our nightly reading (now it's

Obama's *Dreams from My Father*—exquisite), music playing softly, candle burning, and the tender words we say to close the day. Reassuring markers of time.

Kim stood on his own yesterday, holding onto only a 4-legged cane. I'm not sure I saw right, but I swear that Keith (PT extraordinaire) let go of Kim. Perhaps for only a minute, but what a moment in time! It is nothing small to see Kim find his balance, standing 6'3". GORgeous. He then walked to his chair (with support), perhaps 10" away. Both Kim and Keith were sweating after that, but hey, we're talking amazing. I could hardly react, no doubt because I could hardly believe my eyes. I can honestly say that anything is possible with this skilled PT and Kim's undauntable, seemingly inexhaustible desire to work 'til he drops. His hope grows and he seems to pull energy out of places I didn't even know existed.

Yet naps continue and lengthen, as does sleeping late whenever possible. No positive change in eating or voice strength; another barium swallow test last week showed up nothing. I think that's good news, although the difficulties remain. Pain is constant, yet one wouldn't know it by Kim's attitude. Only one seizure, the first in 6 weeks. All in all, a strong couple of months.

Too, we've visited two more delightful third-grade classrooms, the last 'til next school year when we hope to start up again. West Sound Academy's 11th and 12th graders continue to visit us in pairs to discuss their humanities studies and share dreams, brightening our week. I did make it to San Francisco last month to visit my sister; Kim and I handled the separation easily thanks to bro-in-law Kevin and our accomplished caregiver. It was a treat to see my sister, who looked better than ever and kept me laughing and loving.

And I got a job! Four hours a month. "Diversion Monitor" means that I'll coordinate the Diversion boards for Bainbridge. Diversion is the option for teens committing misdemeanors. Youth are given the option of meeting with a group of community volunteers rather than going to court and sitting before a judge. The Board listens to them and their parents, asks questions to "seed" change, and then metes out consequences for healing and learning, not punishment. Kim and I have volunteered on the Board since 2005 and will continue to do so. I'm thrilled for this window into the wider world, for this is the work I must do in the world. Too, I can see all sorts of possibilities coming from this, from deeper conversations with other Board members to having a platform for activism. Ah, trust in how the world works.

I loved your responses to the wisdom of third-graders I put into the last update. I cannot top that, yet for a bit of humor I can pass on Kim's latest idea to do a YouTube video of disgusting noises. Imagine (or not). Then there's our handle: "I've been down so long..." with endings such as "I've been down so long that going to the carwash is an adventure." No lack of finding humor in our new life. It keeps us chuckling.

Elsewhere in the world are sorrows hitting us hard. Our sweet, generous and beautiful friend died last week after a struggle with cancer. My heart is with you and your loving partner as you journey. Pure hearts, souls that inspire. Prayers are with another old friend who is working against all odds to handle what her body is putting her through. And an elder who has been in my life for decades is nearing her time. I'm witnessing life from birth to death and beyond. It's in our face, perhaps more clearly than ever.

Could it be our age? Are we at that place where our friends pass on? I always thought that that happened "later." Yet there's something in this dramatic time that is raw yet important; may I keep perspective.

I go to the natural world for my understanding. Birds are slowly returning to our deck—hallelujah! YES, garden is growing; flowers continue to stun and delight. The warmth returning to the days is so welcomed. The circle continues. I breathe deeply. May you too find yourself in a garden of beauty.

With much care and love, ~ Judy

Being by the water always brought out our good humor.

July 4, 2009

Today is the fourth of July. We just passed through half of 2009. It's been 1 year and 3 seasons since Kim's stroke. Nine years since my mother passed away. A young neighbor just turned one. Two months 'til Kim is 69. So many birthdays, weddings, and anniversaries to celebrate. I seem to be taken with marking time, perhaps to keep perspective on where we are right now.

Time sure baffles me. Our days fly by, weeks too. I often lose track of what day it is, lose track of the conveyor-belt notion of time. I am living in a spiral, a wave, a cyclical space. It is becoming the norm rather than an elusive concept. I like it here—no urgency to move forward. Rather, it is my breath that guides me, and my work is to stay on the belly of the wave and flow with.

Except that I'm aging! That is part of the flow, I see, and I have to let go of the image of the younger woman I once was. I think I can get away with keeping the spirit of that woman intact, but I have a lot to adjust to. Kim says we should outlaw mirrors. (There is that upside of not being able to see well.) Finding our sense of self from within, forget who is peering back at you in the reflection.

Kim wants to tell you what he sees, what he pays attention to. If not in this update, he will soon. I can tell you that he is doing well, working intensely hard at physical therapy as well as always being up for friends. Too, we've successfully wheeled onto the ferry and off, landing in the heart of Seattle: yet another freedom. (Okay, Seattle friends, get ready for a downtown rendezvous!) We're headed to the Olympic Music Festival tomorrow, an idyllic concert-in-the-barn setting for exquisite chamber music. Last month I was the graduation speaker for West Sound Academy's seniors, honored to be asked; it was truly one of the high points of my life. I loved being able to speak from my heart and bless these radiant kids as they embark on their journey. We keep stretching our comfort zone. Lovely baby steps, and we wake with energy.

Yet I must also tell you that a month ago Kim had an anxiety attack and seizure followed by some seriously high fevers. Best guess is that it was a lymph infection. It came out of the blue (where does that phrase come from, I wonder?) and took us by surprise. That is behind us now, yet his pain continues unabated—mostly behind his right eye where the surgery was and in spasms in his left paralyzed leg. His trauma therapist is working with him to objectify pain, to get some distance from it, give it a shape and a color, and to stay curious and unguarded. She's teaching us to place pain outside ourselves and not be controlled by it, to choose to focus elsewhere. Kim came up with a powerful image of his pain being the continent of Africa, the tip being the Cape of Good Hope. We were there; it's a deep visceral feeling for him. He is learning to rest in his heart, free from pain and at peace.

Peace in our hearts. We're happy and remain utterly grateful. How fortunate we are to be surrounded by so much care and to feel so meaningfully engaged in life! That's perhaps the biggest thing I've learned so far as I begin to participate in a 3-month research project through Kent State U in Ohio. They are looking at online support for spouses of stroke survivors; it promises to be worthwhile.

Summer is here in earnest. We're now in temperatures up to 90—hot for us. Our garden is a hoot. We just ate the first broccoli, peas are almost gone, tomatoes are in flower, beans are 7" and are reaching up and over the front door, squash is nearly bite-size, beets are ready and onions too, and cucumbers are about to climb. Birds are plentiful: The brilliant yellow of the goldfinch still surprises me, and crossbills came through last week. None are bathing in the solar birdbath yet; I'll let you know when to get the binoculars out.

We keep mighty active with many visitors already this season, spicing up our lives. There is always something sweet hidden in the freezer ready for an instant party. Please feel welcome. We'll be here.

Wishing us all a peaceful and bountiful summer. Thanks so much for being close by.

Love, ~ Judy

Dear Kim,

I was thinking this morning that it seems that in the lives of the best teachers, it ceases to be something they do and becomes something they are. These people plant themselves so solidly within the cycle of learning and sharing, sharing and learning, that it becomes an essential aspect of themselves.

I see that teaching spirit in both my mom and you—both lifelong teachers who have left the classroom but wherever they find themselves, constantly learning and constantly teaching. You are the essential people who call us over, ask us about ourselves, our thoughts, and where we'd like to go, who love to learn what's possible in the physical world and the world of ideas, and who delight in sharing it. Where you've been (dear Kim!), you've been learning and teaching. And what a gift that's been and will continue to be.

Much love, Tallie

P.S. You helped me decide to try teaching as a profession. Even though I wanted to teach, I was afraid that I would become dowdy, rule-oriented, narrow-minded if I became "a teacher," so I always used to use you as my counterexample to the stereotypical teacher in my head. I said the myself, "Look at Kim! He's not any of those things you're worried about," and filled out the damned applications.

Two of the things I learned from observing you being a teacher that I think about as I teach: (a) be an interesting and interested person and you'll have a better shot at being an interesting teacher and (b) learn to ask great questions. (And c) be a goofball, cut apple slices as thinly as you can, love the ocean and boats, travel intelligently and compassionately, know how to make yourself laugh, drink tea from a thermos when you have to be outside in the cold, and enjoy people, music, and food at all costs.

Kim working in the Democratic Republic of Congo with a young man named Innocent.

Part 8
Grief and Praise

This year has been full of wonder. We've added in Kim's afternoon teas with students, where he's clearly doing more than teaching history. We have returned to volunteering with Diversion, guiding youth who are tangling with the law. And Kim is loving his time with third-graders in raising awareness about the "ability" in disabilities. To top it off, Kim is managing to walk! Yes, with support at his side and a cane, yet the freedom he must feel has to be unequaled.

And yet the grief is intense, for both of us. The dips are getting deeper now. We both have moments of confusion, of anger, of frustration, of pain—of course. Seems the lesson is that there is nothing to do but to breathe and witness. We hold onto gratitude for what has remained undiminished, such as the grace surrounding us and the power of love.

August 11, 2009

We've hit a rough patch. No, not physically as Kim is holding steady, even getting stronger. We are working diligently on smoother transfers to enable us to take to the road without worry and are slowly getting more confident. We've also found that acupuncture can do some magic with Kim's headaches; we'll gladly keep following that thread.

Rather, it's the emotional and spiritual realms that have ensnared us. It seems that as we near the 2-year mark since Kim's stroke, the reality of his situation is becoming clearer, and it is painful. He is filled with grief and anger. How could that not be the case? In my efforts to help comfort, I've taken on the voice of reality, a voice that is not readily received.

Kim is confused and frustrated over why he is not being offered a contract at West Sound Academy. He so wants to teach! Forget the logistics of handling a classroom of kids, planning, reading essays, and crafting tests, let alone getting there on time each day; he loves being in the classroom and feels slighted. I can talk with him at length about how he teaches me, us all, each and every day…about ways he can continue to work with teens (and third-graders)…the many other ways to be involved both in our cohousing community as well as on the Island…but it does not seem to soothe him.

Then there is his beloved peapod, the boat he built nearly 30 years ago and rowed to Alaska. This sweet boat has been such a huge part of his life. As Kim hasn't been able to repair it these last few years, it is at a point where it needs major attention. I think he is choosing to keep it alive rather than let it return to the soil, yet that means letting it go. We are hoping that the Port Townsend Wooden Boat Foundation and the new Maritime Center will adopt it, taking on the repairs and adding it to their livery for use in their education programs. This feels like the best possible option to me, keeping it "in the family" as we both have so many friends in Port Townsend. It would mean that I (and you) could row it as well. To keep the story alive, Kim is in the process of writing memoirs of his boat, speaking into his iPod with me transcribing. I cannot know how hard it must be for him to love it enough to let it go.

Last night he got upset that summer is coming to a close and we have not yet made it to the ocean. It's true. We have been taking increasingly longer trips, but I wouldn't say they have been successful. Between his not traveling in the car well, his limited energy, and my anxiety over toileting, it becomes almost too much for me. Sometimes I think we should just go, regardless of the outcome. I, who once was quite the risk-taker (I married Kim, for example), am now constantly on alert for any dangers. I take so seriously the responsibility I have for this utterly dependent, precious love.

I know we will get through this time. I need to take deeper breaths and trust in this healing process. Grief comes differently for each of us and must come in its own time. I know our spirits are strong and that we are laden with inner resources. I know too that if we didn't love and feel so deeply, grief would not have a place.

So, again, I look to the birds for hope. I wake to the musical chirps of no less than a dozen pine siskins, chickadees, and goldfinches feeding noisily. YES, they are bathing, hallelujah! Their antics continue to draw me outward and up.

Please know that you need do nothing other than hold us in your thoughts and hearts. Your priceless support helps us through the days. Wishing us all a bountiful, beautiful close of summer.

With love, ~ Judy

Top: Kim building his peapod on Lummi Island, Washington, 1980.
Middle left: Young Kim grew up on the water. Middle right: Never far from a boat as a teen.
Bottom left: Kim loved the boat he built, often "repairing" it with duct tape.
Bottom right: The Eileen R *found her final home at the Northwest Maritime Center in Port Townsend, Washington. Kim is with friend Joe Arnett.*

September 14, 2009

We're doing well, drinking in the sunshine and gobbling up the sweet air. What a summer! The bit of rain and cold we had a few weeks back sobered us and also added to our appreciation of the warmth we have now. Not to mention the abundant harvest that is still going strong. Come by for fresh beans, beets, tomatoes, cucumbers, juicy pears, and crisp apples.

We've been doing well, really well. Kim's peapod is happily in Port Townsend and was the star at the brand-new Maritime Center during this weekend's Wooden Boat Festival. We'll soon find out if folks have signed on to help with the repair, guided by the skilled shipwright, Kees. We plan to go there as well, for Kim can sand the planks while he plies us with stories.

In spite of challenges, our trip to PT went beautifully. It was our first overnight, a wonderful reward for Kim's hard work. Besides delivering the boat to its new home, we met up with treasured friends from my life there in the '90s. Friends Joe and Mimi joined us and helped out in every way, including creating a party atmosphere in Room 101, aided by wine, song, and laughter. We stayed at the Tides Inn, right on the water, complete with ornate bedposts and lamps in the shape of 3" ceramic sirens with lampshades as hats. I was in heaven, rising early the next morning to sit with the herons and watch the sun slowly spread across the water. The trip was quite the proof of Kim's continued healing and strength.

With sister Susie and brother-in-law Kevin, 2006.

In fact, we're planning one more trip before the weather closes in—to Leavenworth on the other side of the mountains. Kim's sister Susie and her husband Kevin will come out from Massachusetts the last weekend of September, and we plan to drive east to catch the yellow tamarack and see the salmon run, as well as meet up with friends in this quaint Bavarian town. I relish even the idea of it (the drama of crossing the mountain pass!) and am pleased that we are both up for the journey.

We have yet to plug into schools, though we remind ourselves that it is still early September and a lot can happen. Staying hopeful as well as resourceful.

Two years on the 23rd: a time to reflect and remember how far we've come. I figure the first year was about survival, the second has been about figuring out how to manage life—and we've gotten good at it. This third year is a time for enriching our days yet more, adding in some of the luxuries to feed our souls. We continue to be exquisitely companioned by so many friends and love sharing our food and quiet space with you.

Another blessing is that Kim is sleeping through the night. At least he has this past week and I dare hope it'll continue. I think we can credit a lot of that to our marvelous acupuncturist, Annie, whose magic seems to be holding. I'm catching up on sleep and am learning that I can feel replenished when I feed my creative side: nature, music, arts, and languages.

I've been picking up my guitar (although I honestly haven't gotten better since 6th grade). We're singing! Nothing thrills me as much as hearing Kim's voice meet mine. I told him last night it's as close as I get to the feeling I have when we row together, he pulling steadily and powerfully behind me. Together we are that much stronger. I'm also in touch with a harp teacher and hope to take a lesson or two and will hold out hope to find time to paint again. We've begun meeting with a cohousing neighbor to converse in Spanish each week. And we continue with our small sangha here on Tuesday nights, for mindfulness and meditation is at the core of our ability to keep perspective and find peace in what is.

So yes, this house is rocking with music again, filled with fresh garden veggies and ready for conversation. We hold everything lightly, knowing that the pattern in the Universe is one of waves, not points. Yet we celebrate this moment in time, and always with a sweeping awareness that we are part of a very large and incredibly wonderful circle of friends.

With blessings to all as we welcome the autumn.

Love, - Judy

November 22, 2009

"Summoned by a stroke." That's the phrase that came to me two years ago; tonight, I think I understand it. Kim has been summoned by this stroke to be his highest self. A mere life of global living and activism wasn't enough. He needed this monumental challenge to draw out the full depth of his being. He continues to amaze and delight; his sense of play and compassion both are at a zenith.

Kim fell asleep tonight saying he is at peace, contented, happy. He is loving himself. How can this be? Maybe you can help us understand. One would think otherwise, given the trauma and lessons he has had to live through. There is a passage in *The Snow Leopard* by Peter Matthiessen where the lama living isolated high up on a craggy mountainside, although going blind and lame, is happy. When asked how that could be so when he has so few options, he answers, "Ah, but that is precisely why I am so happy!" I'm beginning to get it.

I am living with a master at accepting what is, living fully, loving openly with a heart as wide as the world. I watch Kim greet everyone with kindness and attention, shining his full presence on them. It is powerful. He has no bitterness. He still loves to be the center of attention (luckily so) and can so easily laugh at himself. He is irreverent and funny. Kim's the steady one in the family; I feel well taken care of.

So yes, we are in good shape to head into winter. Kim continues to get stronger. I wish I could accurately describe how he walks with Keith, his wonderful physical therapist. Keith has figured out that Kim does best with a waltzing pattern: taking 3 small steps with his right leg, then drawing his left leg to the right (leaning on a cane and with Keith holding up his left side). Kim's left leg responds, although he may not feel it beneath him. The air outside was so beautiful a few weeks ago that they were waltzing on the outside deck. There was something about the wind in Kim's hair and the rhythm of his gait that brought tears to my eyes. That man works so hard, so intently. As soon as he landed back in his chair, he said, "Let's do more!" I know why I love him.

There is something Kim would want you to know: He has retired. I don't know what your reaction is, although I'd guess you're surprised. It is pretty clear to most of us that Kim is not able to be a classroom teacher, at least not in the traditional sense. He cannot see, cannot read, could not recognize students raising their hands, couldn't create or grade papers, and his sense of time is lost (hard for an historian). But to Kim, it has been devastating to not have had a contract at West Sound Academy this year. So I finally said that most people his age (69) are happy to retire and to think of the possibilities, how one's world could open up! He could do anything he wants to! He bought it. So now he HAS retired, and sure enough, opportunities have been finding him.

We are in HS classes talking about Africa; we're back with third-graders this year for the disability awareness program on Bainbridge; we're keeping up with Diversion for at-risk youth; and we were the storytellers at church last Sunday with Kim as "Og," a giant helping Noah get the animals on the Ark (yes, I was Noah). He is being skillfully interviewed by Sean Sebastian, a recent graduate from West Sound, who is doing an oral history on Kim for a university class; Sean is drawing out Kim in a way I've never seen. In a week, we'll Skype with a class at Wittenberg University in Ohio, speaking with new teachers learning about disabilities. Phew! I've become his social secretary.

Back to retirement. We've started a "Retirement Book" with entries from those who care to say a few words of how Kim has inspired them and taught them—whether that be in a classroom or in the "school of life." We're adding pictures, too. So please, do consider contributing. You can snail-mail or email a few sentences and a photo, if possible. It's a small book; nothing need be monumental. Kim would be delighted. My goal is that he will never again say that he is not a teacher. I think it's working.

Through all of this, I've had my share of ups and downs. Yet last week something kicked into place, and I'm practicing the art of relaxing into each moment with more faith. (So what if we're late? Who cares if I'm behind on getting this birthday card out?) It's a happier place to be and I'm pleased with us. Kim reminds me to sing when I get anxious, which always soothes.

So as we head into this time of darkness and dreaming, firelight and friendships, and thanksgiving and generosity, we reach out with our hearts in gratitude. Our connections with you, our friends, are the richest part of our lives. We are living a life of abundance. May none of us ever feel alone.

With heartfelt blessings, ~ Judy

December 25, 2009

Here's our holiday present to all—a short clip of Kim walking! No joke. Check this out (yes, it's on YouTube).

If you have trouble with this, please let me know. And now that I'm a bit more techno-savvy (accent on "bit"), I'll try posting a few photos here as well. It's wonderfully exciting to see Kim move so confidently. Too, it seems that this is helping all of him; he's eating better, feeling better, and getting yet more mischievous. So yes, anyone "Got Hope?"

All the best for a wonderful holiday season!

Love, ~ Judy

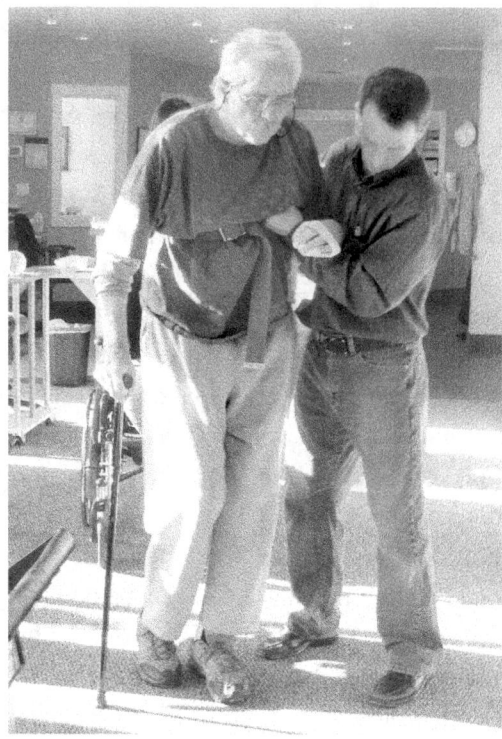

Kim doing the impossible, guided by the incredibly skilled physical therapist, Keith.

March 2, 2010

I know it's been a while since I've written, a sign of full lives with (happily!) little drama. For those of you tracking, thank you for paying such close attention. No need to worry as I promise to report anything of interest immediately.

We just celebrated two years at home: remarkable. I could not have imagined how rich and engaged our lives would become. Thank you too for your sweet comments on our "Kim's Walking!" YouTube clip. He has gotten stronger since then, now 2 months ago, prancing gracefully and walking further each week. Kim now stands outside at our deck railing, waiting for someone to drive by so he can wave. For those of you familiar with Sherman Alexie's *Smoke Signals*, you get the picture.

As Kim gets stronger, we get busier. We have 7 third-grade disability-awareness programs this winter and we're now welcoming West Sound Academy high-school students for tea each week. We both are delighted to be around young folks, especially teens, and cherish our connection. Third-graders continue to surprise us with their open eyes and curious minds. Our favorite question was "What's your favorite toy?" Ha! That a nine-year-old would want to know! Sure got us thinking. (Kim's is the pink lobster he dangles for our cat.) And yours?

Our cohousing community continues to be extraordinary support as well as conspirators in fun. Since the first of the year, we've been calling "Song Circles" almost every week. That's been magic. Music has a way of chasing away the blues and bringing in spirit. Kim's singing voice is stronger than his speaking voice; he closes his eyes and croons. Plays harmonica too, wonderfully well. There's more—from "Winter Wanderlust" travel programs each month to keep us dreaming to our "Heart Circle" for quiet conversation in our home. It is lovely to be here and be able to create circles of trust and sharing. We're involved as well as with our Unitarian Universalist community, and now we're the reps for the branch of UU working globally for human rights. Our last article for the monthly newsletter was about ways of being an activist, even from a wheelchair.

A few other tidbits: Kim's peapod rowboat is in Port Townsend getting repaired. We went to visit it a few weeks ago and thanked all those involved in caring for her, especially Joe, who somehow finds time to add his skills. Kim's been working on his memoirs of the *Eileen R*, pulling out old and crystal-clear memories of that time, now 30 years ago. He does read his Kindle, although his eyesight isn't any better. He's accepted that too. Eating, though, is fine. Food (still!) is surely the way to his heart.

Then of course, there is the unmistakable change in the air. Sweet smells from the hyacinths, Michiko's azalea across the path bursting forth in lavender blooms, birds tunneling through the sunny seeds. The garden has begun in earnest. Sugar snap and snow peas, radishes, and onions planted. The vision of lushness is set, energy is high, and the earth feels so delicious.

It does amaze me how much Kim and I can share. We love doing things together. Perhaps we're growing more like each other, as we've (had to) become inseparable. Our respect for the other doesn't waiver; our love is steady and forgiving and compassionate.

Yet I want to find a way to say that as we get busier, there IS a trade-off. More activities seem to come with more expectations. Funny how it's almost harder to stay in gratitude when we have more. Counterintuitive. We pull each other back to stay present rather than jump at the next event or goal. Time to celebrate each accomplishment. People often ask where Kim's walking will lead. I say, "right here." For one, we don't know what is possible. He has already far surpassed anything I had imagined. For another, it's painful when we aren't satisfied with what is. Like chasing dust bunnies, we neither settle nor find peace. We can't go deep if we don't go slow. We are lucky to have that luxury to live a little slower and honor each day.

So, our practice continues to be the same: staying in the moment with full awareness, attention, and gratitude. May we keep open our hearts to each person we encounter. Seneca reminds us that "Wherever there is a human being, there is an opportunity for kindness." So many of our friends are facing loss, illness, and hard times as well as new life coming. Seasons of life.

The news that reaches us from afar is distressing. Reason enough to stay grounded in what we know today. We reach out as we are able and are now strong enough to give back. Please do call on us, do visit, and do share stories of adventures and conundrums and "wise fool" anecdotes. We'll have some to pass on as well!

With love to you and your family as we journey together. ~ Judy

June 18, 2010

These past months continue to be perhaps the calmest, least dramatic time of my life. It feels almost odd. Kim remains steady and quite predictable in his energy (not in his humor, luckily!), and I've found a balance, incredible as that is. Although we hang out in our little tree house of a home most of the time, our lives are full of adventure (relatively speaking) and deepening friendships, culinary surprises, and unexpected events. The birds are like teenage boys in their feeding frenzy; the garden is slow this year though the sweet peas are keeping us patient. Plenty to keep on top of right here within arms' reach.

Kim's walking continues to blow me away. You saw the YouTube clip I posted last Christmas? Well now it's 6 months later and Kim is moving. "Not enough Os in "smooooth," as Martha would say. Keith hands Kim over to me and we waltz the length of the PT room. Judging by Kim's exhaustion at the end of the hour, I'd say it's akin to climbing Mt. Everest. His perseverance and focus are something to behold. And how I love looking UP at him. Ha! He is beautiful.

Our health has been exceptional. Only a few weeks of vertigo for Kim but no seizures. I've almost forgotten what they are like. Kim still has wild headaches, yet he manages to sleep well. I've had some bouts with bugs that, I guess, decide I'm too tough a character to camp out here for long.

Speaking of character, we have been feted once again. The senior class at West Sound Academy chose to give us a "Character Award" as a couple. It is the first-ever, and the story is that from here on, the award will be named after us. Goodness! How can this be? The acknowledgment we get continually for just living is unbelievable.

I bow to generosity. I don't understand it, don't need to. I Believe. The more I can let flow through me, through us, the richer we are. That be things, thanks, thoughts, even money. We act on any positive impulse that rises, reside in kindness. It comes back many times over.

Family, for one. We are blessed with bimonthly visits from Kim's daughter Megan in tow of her 5-year-old son Henry, accompanied by her mother Judy and Chihuahua Polly. We've had visits from cousin Sandy from New Jersey…and recently from sister Susie from Massachusetts. I've taken a day to fly to see my sister Alice in San Francisco. Wonderful, memorable visits, all. Friend Damon came out from the East Coast, Mary and Cliff up from New Mexico, and Seattleites make the splendid effort to ferry across the pond. Island neighbors haven't slowed down in their invites either; we have an ongoing list of friends to visit. Yet I hold Kim's nap time sacred. It's my few hours of quiet, too, and we both need the rest. Thank you for understanding if our dance card seems full.

In our sweet community, our monthly Song Circles seem to have caught hold, and we hosted a tremendous digital storytelling workshop that Greg Tuke gave, coming over from Seattle "just because." We're planning a tide-pool trip next month on the Olympic Peninsula to my all-time favorite marine preserve. Too, Kim and I are putting our hearts and energy into finding ways to welcome our eclectic group of 7 young cohousing teens into community a bit better. We love living here, happy with this nest of care and connection. We venture out for concerts, plays, and movies; Bainbridge is entertainment-rich.

We're even working! A few high school classes this past year; never enough for Kim. We cherish our time with these thoughtful, curious, engaged youth. It is now a year since I've taken on the coordinator role for the Diversion program on Bainbridge. Kim joins me once a month as part of our volunteer community board, helping to guide youth in trouble with the law. Also very exciting for me is a new friend who has asked that I mentor her in mediation. She is stunning in spirit and wise in experience, and I already cherish our connection. It's good to feel part of my old life returning.

We watch friends around us go through life passages of birth, graduation, moving, illness, death—and extend a hand as we can. Life is fleeting; we remind each other to hold everything lightly. The news details things unimaginable, yet another nod to how privileged we are. I'll even accept the cold rainy weather we've been having for how grateful I am to have such natural beauty around me.

The only downside of such ease is that I haven't been feeling especially reflective. The injustice of it all! It takes drama and trauma to bring out the poet in me!! Ah, but the lessons never stop. I balance only when I can stay in this moment: the past causes grief, the future anxiety. So here I perch when I remember, right here, the "sweet spot" of life. It is worth it. We're happy.

For when we reach too far in either direction, we lose the grace. With expectations come more opportunities to be disappointed. I call it "eagle-ing" when either one of us holds onto something so tightly that we might drown with the weight of what we want. (Eagles can drown if they grasp a fish that is strong enough to pull it under.)

Back to this moment and the elegance of gratitude. Like the old lama living in the craggy mountainside that Peter Matthiessen describes in *The Snow Leopard* who is happy precisely because he has no options.

So, friends, we thank you. We don't forget for a minute that you are journeying with us, as we are with you. Please keep in touch.

With love and joy, ~ Judy

Daughter Megan and grandson Henry giving Kim a high five at his physical therapy session.

AUGUST 16, 2010

It's time to celebrate a birthday coming up. Yup, Kim's. Wanna guess how old? Ha! The Big Seven-Oh! 9/9/1940, and he is going strong.

I think it's time to roast him. Kim's been getting so many accolades and honors lately, so how about some of those juicy stories? The kind that will draw out a belly laugh? Please, do send me some (in secret) and we'll be sure to read them aloud—with the appropriate drama!—on his birthday: Thursday, September 9th. We'll do up a cake with all the trimmings at, 7:30 here at our cohousing Common House, for those of you who are local and can make it. Our devoted friends Archie and Tejavani will be driving over from Missoula, MT. Kim doesn't want a lot of fuss, so we'll go for quality.

Our summer has been humming along. This week has been hot; he almost wore shorts. I've been teasing him about getting a "lederhosen tan" with his high socks. We have our own version of ups 'n' downs yet seem to come out on the crests.

We think of you, our comforting and inspiring circle of friends and family, and thank you for holding the space for us to live each day.

With love, ~ Judy

A more humorous than helpful scene at a cohousing retreat.

PART 9
SACRED TIME

Three years now, and there's a rhythm to our new normal. We still mourn the "old Kim" while celebrating the "new Kim." I may not have mentioned that, though the "old" Kim and I have been married for many years, this "new" Kim proposed to me a bit ago—and I accepted heartily. I am so glad that there's such a resemblance between the two, for I love them both!

Yet I think the first of fall will always summon a visceral angst in me. I feel it now. The moment of Kim's stroke is lodged in my body; it remembers. The smell and colors of this season pull out my grief as well as my tenderness. This is sacred time.

SEPTEMBER 23, 2010

The first of fall. School starting. Kim's 70th birthday. The maple outside our window turning scarlet. Rosh Hashanah and a new year. Three years since Kim's stroke, today.

There is something powerful about anniversaries, I'm convinced. This one feels all-encompassing, demanding my attention. Three years: a "lifetime," yet a blink. Kim said last night that he is more contented than he has ever been in his entire life. Imagine! I'll ask him to explain more and then pass his secret on to you. What a teacher. And me? In grief. It comes and goes, yet today I cannot ignore the tumultuous change that has impacted our lives and dreams.

Our days continue to pass unbelievably quickly and cheerfully. We remain very engaged with our community as well as with the broader world. We just started a "Homework Club" for the students (young and old) in our community; next week I'll do my best to start teaching guitar to a handful of teens. Ha! Stretching all the time. We're also on the verge of diving into some HS classrooms; third-grade disability awareness is around the bend. To top it off, we've been asked to facilitate 3 short classes on Judaism for middle schoolers at our Unitarian Universalist church.

There is so much for me to learn, finally growing in understanding of the religion into which I was born. I'm loving this opportunity.

Yes, we're still keeping up with Diversion, supporting "at-risk" youth and parents; also meeting others on the Island who work with teens. I am so drawn to this work. It is the one thing that pulls me out of myself, challenges and delights me. Actually, Kim and I both; we must have something in us that knows that being around young people rekindles our spark.

Kim keeps working his body 'til he drops. Keith (our extraordinary physical therapist) said last Monday that Kim has now surpassed his expectations. He gave us homework: to walk 100 steps each day. And we do, 'round the bed. Fuji just lies there on her princess mountain of blankets and purrs; she seems to like the cadence of Kim's steps and cane, and my whispered encouragements.

Neighbor Maggie leading the way in style, back from a frozen yogurt outing.

So yes, we're doing a lot. Yet we're also "being." I think we are living better than we ever have: conscious of how we spend our time, always choosing kindness and generosity, leaving nothing left unsaid, doing anything loving we can think up, and holding things lightly. I've had a clear glimpse of how life now feels more cyclical with each day deepening, rather than a conveyor belt where we try to get somewhere. Rest and reflection time we intentionally hold sacred.

We remain ever committed to, and grateful for, our neighbors who offer unending support, time, gifts of presence, and the little things that smooth out our day. Our family afar keeps in close touch; Megan (Kim's daughter) surprised us on his birthday! She was The Gift. And our solid, caring circle of friends never ceases to amaze us. So there alongside grief is gratitude.

May the beauty of this time of year fill us all with clarity and abundance. It's the time I long to be in the northeast woods, smelling the air and witnessing the striking change in the leaves. We know of many changes affecting some of you too; we hold you in our hearts and send wishes for healing.

Blessings to all. ~ Judy

P.S. Kim is not yet able to explain why he feels so at peace, yet I think I know. It is love. That and playfulness! We are stronger together than ever, a miracle in itself.

December 2, 2010

Something is happening here. I can no longer deny or ignore it. This life keeps moving; they say one cannot step into the same river twice. Kim has not felt well for weeks; he has been sleeping a lot and eating very little. A few weeks back he had a low-grade fever and chills, possibly a virus. We went to the clinic three Saturdays running, and again in between for an ultrasound on a bump on his leg (most likely a hematoma). Many mysteries, for they could find nothing amiss in all the tests they ran.

Kim says he's tired. Physically tired. Says he wants to rest. I know he is tired emotionally, too. Although I watch him unending, I cannot find words for what it must take for him to just get up in the morning or rally for friends and activities, let alone for walking. His strength and spirit are unfathomable; his humor remains intact. This stroke has brought out qualities from Kim's depths that may have stayed hidden living a "normal" life. My love for him overflows.

I feel like I'm in a twilight zone, feeling the earth shift as I stand still. Always, these lessons of "Be Here Now" and staying fully present. When crisis hits, I get closer to the ground, gain balance from the earth and sky. I am steady enough when I hold things lightly.

We are as loving as ever, patient and kind with each other. We talk, deeply and intimately. We are life partners forever. I don't know where this will take us. What I do know is that I will never leave Kim's side.

Please don't treat us any differently. Know that we are choosing to live quieter and have cut back on many activities. It is time for the spirit to take over, to not push up mountains. We are at peace.

And we need your support. Nothing outward, just your blessings. We are being courageous as we slowly move toward this next unknown chapter of our lives.

With deep gratitude, and love. ~ Judy

DECEMBER 21, 2010

A solstice greeting to all, and cheerful news that Kim is doing much better! He is eating again and gaining strength. We're not back to physical therapy or outside activities, although we're now beginning to have the energy to welcome friends dropping by.

I think Kim realized that there are still lots of foods he wants to eat before he checks out. He's been asking for Greek pizza, Raisin Bran, turkey sausage pasta, pumpkin scones, even a McDonald's Big Mac. I indulge him silly. It's great to have my playmate back in humorous form.

Perhaps more than the physical nourishment, I believe Kim's spirit is back because of your steady support, outpouring of care, and blessings…

…just in time for the holidays. Here's to a celebration of the light returning, along with wishes for us all to find peace in heart and home, and the strength to be open to what the New Year will bring.

With love, ~ Judy

MARCH 7, 2011

Nearly a season has passed since I last wrote. Goodness! Guess that's a sign that we're steady and too, that days melt into each other. How can I explain why I seem to find so little time to reflect and write? It is nearing midnight as I type this. Kim is sleeping soundly, and our sweet kitty is by my side. I love the stillness at the end of a day.

We've crossed our 3-years-at-home mark, still amazed and grateful at our good fortune to have had this cozy home to move to. Add another half- year since Kim's stroke. Hard to fathom. Cohousing continues to feed us in many ways: I know we have the best kids and teens anywhere, as well as the unbelievable care and support of so many neighbors.

Kim IS back at physical therapy, and proudly so. He has nearly recouped what he lost last fall. It takes my breath away, still, to see how intensely hard he works just to stand, let alone walk. It is terrifically important to him; no one needs to nudge him to put out. This little island is home to exceptional healers, and somehow, we have found them.

And I've managed to do the impossible, leaving overnight for a full 24 hours away. Thanks to the 3 caregivers and many friends who took over, and especially to Kim who flexed with it all. I went to Port Townsend for a harp festival and was totally blown away being surrounded by 42 harps and harpists! Heaven, I think. I'm fully inspired and have dreams of knowing this instrument as an intimate part of me, now working (slowly) on some Latin dances. I cannot help but be happy while I play.

We continue to welcome friends and family from far and near who fill our home with laughter and music. The farthest: Andy and Susan from Maine, Kim's buddy from university days. The youngest: little Finn, 9 months old with his mother (Kate, our niece) and his grandmother (Susie, Kim's sister from MA). Many of you make the 2–4 hour round trip just to spend a few hours with us; we know what it takes to carve that time out and we thank you deeply. We've had the pleasure of having our 20-something friends, once teens we taught or mentored, come by during school breaks. It's a gift to journey with you as you grow and find your way in the world! We love it all. You bring energy, news, memories, play, and inspiration.

Being engaged in the community, island-wide as well as global, is as important to us as ever. We continue working with teens through Diversion…continue with the third-graders for the disability awareness program…and I've just taken an ESL tutor training with the hopes that Kim and I can work with English-learners here on the island.

Here's a comment from a parent of a third-grader from the disability program:

I want to express my great appreciation to you. When I picked up my daughter C from school yesterday, she talked at length about the guests you had come speak and teach kids. She even knew their names, Kim and Judy, as if they are old friends. Whatever happened in C's world yesterday, at school, was very big.

"Thank you for bringing in such valuable lessons and opportunities to expand. Humanity. Empathy. Community. That's just a start. My heart was full listening to C tell me that it has been very difficult for Kim, after his stroke, but that he has found ways to live fully. She knew that he was in rehab for 5 months ("that's a long time" she told me). She knew that Kim loved to read and his eyes don't work as well anymore.

"Again, thank you. Hugely. Love really is the whole point.

As the world news brings hope alongside tragedy, we are sobered by the horrific reality for so many people, as well as by our often unacknowledged and unappreciated privilege. There is no way to balance it, make it right. We end up giving more money to causes, writing more letters, and signing more petitions, yet I think the most immediate and impactful thing we can do is to be increasingly aware of our blessings and to live as generously as we can. May kindness radiate outward. Our hearts keep opening.

We're making it through a grey winter, soon to have the freedom to sit in the sun and turn the garden soil. Bulbs are pushing through; Kim notices that the birches are changing color. And we have new life happening close to us! Kim's daughter, Megan, is due with a second son in a few weeks. We love our family and are extraordinarily lucky to have them come here from Brooklyn as often as they do. Henry, now 6, will no doubt be a wonderful big brother. It promises to be a most memorable spring.

So there you have it. Nothing boring about our lives though we hardly leave home. Although I think we've lost some of the edge that comes when thinking these weeks could be our last, I do feel that we will never lose a sense of gratitude for each day. Kim is a joy and endlessly fascinating to me. We remain happy and loving and astounded that this is so.

In peace, ~ Judy

MAY 22, 2011

Trick question: "How many Kimberly Bushes are there in the world?" Answer: "TWO!!"

I've been remiss. I haven't told you. Megan, Kim's daughter, had a second son almost two months ago on March 25th—and she named him Kimberly Samuel Bush! What an honor (I told Kim he'll have to coach the little guy on being a male Kim). It seems that Henry (now 6) is a very happy Big Brother. All seem to be doing swimmingly. Megan has hardly taken time off from work to bring this little spirit into the world. And her equally amazing mother, Judy, has been living with them in Brooklyn to help out. I'd guess she is indispensable.

To make up for my delinquency, I thought I'd try to upload some pictures. If this works, watch out! I may be unstoppable. (I'm s-l-o-w-l-y backing into the techno 21st century.)

Here at home the drama is less; we're holding pretty steady. I marvel at Kim's spirit and humor, neither of which has abated. He still always wakes up chatty and happy. (Darn! I still haven't learned how to do that!) Food is the elixir of life for him; he eats cheerfully. Kim works as hard as ever, though now it's physical therapy and not construction. Yet he dreams of working: one night he is on a roof, another he is a fireman, and yet another night he is in front of a class. Walking remains the highlight of his week; if you come at an opportune time, you will see us prancing around the kitchen.

Yet Kim's energy IS lessening, although he may deny it. We no longer do morning or evening activities. He is awake perhaps 8 hours a day with a nap in between. This makes it a bit harder to schedule around but it has simply become the "new normal." So it is. We continue to love having people visit—we just have to keep it less of a wild party.

We're still waiting for spring to douse us in its full glory. The garden is started and flowers are resplendent, though the sun has barely come out enough for the bees to wake up. I have to replant the beans as I'm sure the seeds drowned last month. No complaints! For I think of our friends dealing with tornados and earthquakes, tsunamis and drought. I'd invite them all here if I could. I'm intensely happy outside and look ahead to long days of soaking up the rays. We do love this part of the world and feel lucky to live here.

I've been taking good care of myself. We bought a sleeper sofa with a solid mattress so that I can stretch out at night (rather than curl up in the recliner, where I have been sleeping). It's a gift, a comforting one. And I've spent a bit of time with old, cherished friends. (Thank you, Mary and Cliff!) The exceptional young kids surrounding us (seven beauties aged 7 and under) draw me out daily. Last Sunday I was at the bottom of the puppy pile, laughing with abandon. Still playing harp, dreaming of flute, ready to take to the mountains when they open. I bless my body for holding up so well; grateful for each day and amazed at how fast they run into each other.

So, see? We can adjust to whatever life offers us. It is all part of the journey. Kim remains my most loving teacher. We, of course, both have our fall-apart days, yet we know they won't last. Humor reminds us, music sustains us, and love only deepens. Please continue to keep us in your hearts and know that you are the center of our lives. Friendships are what knit memories and meaning into this whole cloth. We are quieter and slower, but no less happy.

With peace, ~ Judy

Left: The second Kimmy Bush!
Right: A happy grandfather with six-year-old Henry and baby Kimmy.

AUGUST 30, 2011

"The urgency of mid-summer is now beginning to relax." A phrase I heard on the radio decades ago has stuck in my mind, for it seems to so beautifully describe what I'm feeling. It is definitely transition time. The vine maples are turning, school starts tomorrow, the morning air is cooler and thicker. It's been beautiful here; we don't take it for granted. I want to share it, for so many of you are dealing with hurricanes, floods, and drought. Not to forget our friends in far-flung places living with war. Please may you be safe.

What a summer it has been! So many highs, like meeting Baby Kimmy. He is beyond beautiful. Calm, too, for he is well-loved. Henry has become an outstanding Older Brother, caring sweetly for Baby K in between running after thrown balls. Megan is a marvel, juggling her life with grace and ease. "The Entourage" has been renamed "The 3-Ring Circus": Megan, an active 6-year-old, Baby K, partner Vincent, mother Judy, and Chihuahua Polly.

We made it up to 5,000 feet at Hurricane Ridge in the Olympic Mountains a few weeks ago, for Kim needed to smell the mountain air. I have no words to describe the freshness, with a hint of wildflowers and snow, of the crisp-though-warm breezes. Kim was beside himself (literally) as he seemed to leave his physical body and be totally present (and awake!) the whole day. We ate snow. We watched the deer graze. We stared at the glaciers and the majestic, craggy peaks. We remembered our many, many hikes through this glorious country. Thanks to you, Barbara, for accompanying us and making it possible.

We also stayed in the low country. We heard the most exquisite live chamber music in a barn on a farm at The Olympic Music Festival, accompanied by best of friends Marcy and Rick. Tchaikovsky was never so dramatic and captivating, farm roosters contributing. Jami Sieber, electric cellist extraordinaire, drew us out at night for an other-worldly concert.

We found new lookouts to which we can wheel. Here in our community, we helped host a house-concert on a sunny afternoon…recited a poem at the Talent Show on July 4th…celebrated Lucile's 96th birthday…organized games at our community's annual Summer Extravaganza event. Our weekly sangha-ette continues, happily. We love our work with teens through Diversion, and I cherish my time with my ESL student from Thailand. Kim initiated the "Jose Cuervo Club" (he is always looking for new members). Ha! I know that it is Kim's twice-weekly workouts at physical therapy with Keith that has given him such vitality. Keith got us to walk into, and out of, an elevator. Sound easy? It was breathtaking; it literally took my breath away.

We've had company almost every day, sharing healthy food, hearty laughter, and conversations that bring forth memories and ask new questions. From farthest away: Sarah and Ray and their huggable 14-month-old twins from Japan. I've known Sarah since she was 9; she is my daughter-of-choice, now giving me the joy of watching her grow ever more radiant as a mother. Evy, Tony, Gabe, and David—my oldest friend from the East Coast and her delightful family; laughter I'll never forget! (Please come back!) Our revered nonagenarian relatives from California, Al and Sue, made a special trip to spend a few days with us; an honor and a joy. Al's brother Rick and his wife Ellen came through as well; such rich conversations and the comfort of years of knowing each other and our histories. Sister Susie and bro Kevin came from Massachusetts over the July 4th weekend and walked the parade with us. Kaaren helped us host a reunion of fellow witnesses for human rights who worked alongside Kim in Guatemala from 2002 to 2003. Seattleites came across the pond, Island friends showed up at our door, and many others kept in close touch.

I call Kim "fly paper." I wheel him into the courtyard or even outside our door and presto! In a matter of minutes, he is surrounded by neighbors. We love living here, every year more so (last month marked our 10th year). Love these kids who come by with home-grown cucumbers or artwork or just looking for cats. I thrive on watching them grow. And sometimes watching them launch and return as stunning adults.

So, there you have it. Life in the fast lane. Just kidding, we sleep a lot. Yet our waking hours are packed full of anything we can think up. Wonderful Linda just introduced us to a "talking book reader," courtesy of the library for the blind, that

Kim is able to work on his own. He is hungry to download every book he's ever known. Another step toward independence.

We just celebrated our 11th wedding anniversary (Rodney, you did a good job!), and 15 years of being together. More sobering is that September 23rd will mark four years since Kim's stroke. And soon Kim will turn 71.

This is where YOU come in. We're planning a Poetry and Pineapple party on Friday, September 9th in the evening, 6:30 to 8:00 p.m. If you're in the neighborhood, please come by! Even if not, we're asking for your favorite poetry. I'm putting together a book for Kim; the pages are 5" x 6". Consider sending us either a hard copy that size for pasting in, or something that I can hand-write in. Kim has written a few poems himself lately; perhaps he'll be up for sharing them in the next post.

I'll end with just a moment of gratitude—for you and your kindnesses to us, for Kim and his loving and play and desire to get up each day, for the bounty of the earth outside our door, and for the ease which life is offering us today. Blessed be.

~ *Judy*

P.S. No excuses for the quality of some of these photos; hope you enjoy them anyway—getting a glimpse of our lives.

Our last trip to Hurricane Ridge in the Olympics to smell the mountains.

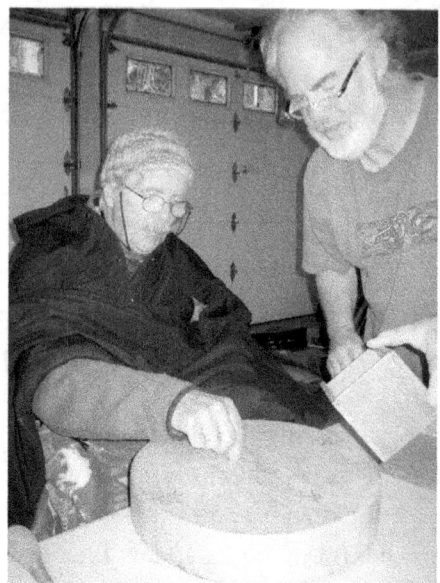

Above left: Shaman John skillfully guiding Kim in building a drum.
Above right: Kim, founder of the "Jose Cuervo Club."

Chiropractor Julie, who believes that laughter helps everything!

PART 10
LETTING GO

We are tired. Intensity takes its toll. I wouldn't change anything, I have no regrets. A fragment of a quote from decades ago has stuck with me: "No one was ever poorer in the long run for having once in a lifetime let out all the length of all the reins." We have, we do, we live every day as if it were our last, for it just might be.

November 2, 2011

Life changes SO FAST. Hang on. Kim is in the ICU once again. We're in a nightmare that started on Halloween and is still picking up speed. I'm back on that edge of being forced to stay in this moment. Right here. For when I get lost in the anxiety of what may happen, I waste precious energy. And I worry about the wrong thing.

Sunday, October 31st, Halloween night. At 9:00 p.m. when Kim was in bed, after I had given out the choco-macaroon spiders with pretzel legs and cinnamon eyes to the tricksters and goblins, he started complaining of severe abdominal cramps. We knew what to do: heat, Gas-X, music. It didn't help. I'm ashamed that I grumbled when he woke me twice more within a few hours on a night when I was especially tired. By the third time, at midnight, I woke fully and called the doc. The pain was becoming unmanageable and Kim started what was to become a 24-hour marathon of hurling. At 1:00 a.m., 911 ambulanced Kim to the emergency room.

After X-rays, scans, and lab tests, the diagnosis was gallstones. At 5 that morning, we were moved to the hospital in Bremerton, 45 minutes down the road, for surgery to remove his gallbladder. It was a horrific day with pain at 9.5 on a scale of 10. The retching continued nonstop. I cannot tell you how Kim held up, and with good spirits too. I am ever in awe of that beautiful husband of mine. Good that we were practiced in patiently waiting, for it wasn't until 7:30 p.m.

Monday night that Kim was wheeled in to surgery. Neither of us had slept since Sunday night. And we were both scared.

The surgeon told me that surgery was successful and more critical than anyone had guessed. Kim's gallbladder was gangrenous, with pictures to prove it. He was quite sick. The harder news was that Kim aspirated the wretched bile and it burned his lungs. He now has "aspiration pneumonia," an acute lung injury.

So here we are in the ICU with Kim on oxygen and fighting to breathe. It's 4:30 Tuesday morning as I write this. There's a chance he'll need a ventilator and feeding tube. I managed to get a wee bit of sleep in the lobby but needed to come back here to hold Kim's hand, the only place that makes sense. Some of my greatest challenges will be to tear myself away to take care of me and to practice not worrying about the wrong things. There's no telling what kind of a ride we're on. Truth is, Kim may be here for a while.

I ask you to please be patient as I return calls and messages; yet, do keep them coming for we need your prayers, your mettā, your blessings, your love. It feels like life is crumbling around me. I think of the monk who is chased by a lion and finds himself hanging off a cliff. The vine he is holding onto is fragile and slowly breaking. He sees a strawberry, reaches for it, and delights in it.

I will keep you informed as we travel this journey. Thank you truly for being there alongside. We cannot do this alone.

With faith in how life unfolds, ~ Judy

Dearest Judy and Kim—

I am so so sorry that the improvement that we've all been praying for has not taken place. I don't have the wisdom to know whether Kim's work here is nearing the end and he gets to go home, but what I do know, I know for sure. You both have lived extraordinarily, you have loved like you'll never get hurt, and you've let go of your former lives as gracefully as a snake sheds its old skin, letting go of all you held dear in order to embrace the "what is" of now. There can be no life lived better, as your "love" has consistently been expressed as a verb rather than a noun. Dear ones, how can I best help? Emmanuel says that when one prays for healing, it's important to understand that death is a form of healing, and that makes so much sense to me except for now, when it's so personal. I will pray rather that you each be given all the strength, hope and light necessary to meet each challenge with faith in the wisdom of the universe, and that love will carry you through each difficulty. As you taught me so many years ago Judy, it's not the body that carries you through the hard times, it's the spirit. You've got spirits that I'm in awe of, and it's important for you to know that many spirits of friends and loved ones are walking with you on the journey…we may not be photogenic, but we are there, and neither of you are alone. I love you both and want you to call, email, or let me know some way if there is anything I (or rather we—Cliff too) can do to lighten the load. Blessed Be.

Mary O'Hern

Taking a moment to reflect on the country Kim so loved, at the tip of South Africa, 2007.

November 4, 2011

Kim is free. He crossed over to the other side early this morning. Peaceful, well-loved, so so ready to go home. I lay in his arms, my favorite place in the world to be.

Please don't be sad for him. He was never sad for himself. May we all honor him by living fully, loving deeply, and practicing each day to let go.

When I get some rest, I/we will figure out how to celebrate Kim's life. I will be sure to let you know.

With immense gratitude for all, especially for having lived the best 15 years one could imagine, with the love of my life.

In peace, ~ Judy

Our last night on our last trip with the Eileen R *at Fay Bainbridge Park, Washington, after circumnavigating Bainbridge Island.*

November 29, 2011

It's now a few days since our celebration for Kim. The last of family and out-of-town guests left this afternoon. The sun has returned after a day or two of rain and blustery winds. And my home is back to quiet and still.

I have to practice saying "my." The reality of this not being one of Kim's corny jokes or extended adventures has yet to hit. It'll take me a while to recognize that this is, indeed, my home and my new life. Alone. Yet Kim's spirit is so much a part of me that he is everywhere, surrounding me. I don't yet fully understand.

You helped make Saturday a stunning day! Thank you for the music, the stories, the food, and for helping in every possible way. Those who couldn't make it sent messages and love. We, together, honored beautifully this dynamic, vital man who lived passionately and touched many souls. Please let us keep telling those stories; I need them. Kim will be laughing along with us.

I have many lessons to live into. One is hitting me especially hard today and it's about being rich. People ask me how I'm managing financially, for neither of us have worked for 5 years when you count our journey to Africa. We can be rich by spending less…and yes, we are good at that, and we have stretched our savings and have been grateful to have them.

Yet what I've learned is that generosity is a way of being that begets more generosity. Counterintuitive. The more we give, the more we receive. Kim taught me that, to give without condition and from the heart. Whatever I can think up. We do, we have, and I am—literally—richer for it.

You have kept us going financially, yet mostly offering support in countless ways. I will continue to pay it forward however I can. I will give all I've got, although what I have changes. Now it's what I've learned about caring for someone I love. I will share that with you when you need it. And I will work again, soon as I figure out who I am after these four transforming years. I do not worry. Please do not worry. We'd only worry about the wrong thing, right?

So this may be my last update on these CarePages. Your messages and your witnessing has sustained me more than I can say. I do not know where my life is headed. I do trust in the way the world unfolds. I trust my journey and the lessons I must learn this time 'round. My work is to stay open and receptive, ready. And to have faith, mostly in myself. I will listen for what calls to me and follow my heart with humility and always with a spirit of generosity. May I be able to stay gracious.

Please stay in touch. Our door is always open and there's always room at the table. Though I don't yet feel like leaving the comfort of my home and kitty, the gypsy in me will no doubt strike again. I love to travel and I will soon know that I am free.

I bow to the mystery of this life. And I thank you, deeply.

In peace, ~ Judy

Epilogue

Here I sit in this sweet tree house of a home that Kim and I shared for most of the four years after his stroke. It is now eight years since he passed over—just the right amount of time for me to gather up my courage and my heart and relay the beauty of the man and the extraordinary journey we shared.

Kim is with me oh-so-often. You can tell when he's near by the smile that forms unbidden or the guffaw that escapes me or the story that just tumbles out. I'm usually laughing, for his effect on me contains joy. And love. He teaches me still and forever. Love is what this time is all about. That lesson serves me well as I stand to face into another day witnessing the confusion and suffering of the world around me.

May we each keep reaching for that river of kindness that connects us all, and live as if each day matters. It truly does.

KIMBERLY BUSH, JR.

September 9, 1940–November 4, 2011

Kim Bush died unexpectedly yet peacefully on November 4, 2011, in the embrace of his wife, Judy. Kim was 71 years old. He was born in New York City on September 9, 1940. He lived at Winslow Cohousing on Bainbridge Island for the last ten years of his life. Kim is survived by his wife Judy Friesem; daughter Megan Bush and grandsons Henry Skeltis and Baby Kimmy Bush of Brooklyn, NY; sister and brother-in-law Susan and Kevin O'Brien of Bolton, MA; and nieces Heather O'Brien of Maynard, MA, and Kate O'Brien of Los Angeles, CA. He also leaves behind a multitude of loving and admiring friends.

Kim was a global citizen and an educator of the humanities for much of his life; he travelled widely. Kim worked in rural development in Tanzania with the Friends Service Committee in the '60s, taught at Cotopaxi International School in Ecuador in the '70s, and directed educational programs in refugee camps in Thailand for the U.N. High Commission for Refugees in the '80s. In the U.S., he taught at Midland School in Los Olivos, California; the Everett School District, and most recently at West Sound Academy (WSA) in Indianola. In June of 2008, his students honored him by dedicating their yearbook to him. And in 2010, WSA students chose to give Kim and his wife, as a couple, the first "Character Award."

A dedicated advocate for human rights, Kim worked tirelessly against apartheid in the '60s and lived nine months in Guatemala in 2002–2003 as an accompanier protecting genocide survivors. He and Judy travelled for seven months in East and South Africa during 2006–2007, offering mediation trainings and connecting with peace builders. In 2007, the Kitsap County Council for Human Rights gave the Lifetime Achievement Award to Kim and Judy for their dedication to peace. Kim had an unending intellectual curiosity and was an avid reader, poet, musician, carpenter, and stone sculptor. He spoke five languages.

Many of Kim's connections to his friends were through their mutual love of nature and outdoor adventures of rowing, cycling, and hiking in the mountains or desert. At age 40, he built a wooden rowing peapod named *Eileen R* after his mother and rowed it to Alaska. Kim remained an avid rower in the San Juan Islands and around Bainbridge, seen year 'round pulling out of Eagle Harbor.

Four years ago, Kim survived a stroke that sliced through his life, bringing an abrupt end to his independence. He was left paralyzed and with compromised vision. Instead of living broadly he now grew roots, planting himself at home surrounded by his cohousing community and friends of all ages who visited from near and far. Although the horizons of his life were diminished, he creatively stretched into what he could do rather than mourn his limitations, always pushing the limits and surpassing the common experience. The stroke summoned his indomitable spirit revealing his patience, kindness, generosity, and considerable humor. He became his highest self and lived abundantly in connectedness with the natural and human world. Kim stayed actively involved in his community, serving the Bainbridge Library Board; sitting on the Diversion Board working with at-risk youth; visiting third-grade classrooms to foster awareness of disabilities; and continuing to mentor high school students. Perhaps most profound was his light-hearted presence of joy and play, and his graciousness toward others. He was grateful for being alive. While his friends were of many traditions, Kim found nourishment in a decades-long Buddhist meditation practice.

Kim's passing is a deep loss to the many people who loved him. He lived passionately and boldly, valuing adventure over ease and friendships above all. May his inspiration to live fully and love deeply remain with us.

Remembrances can be made to Amnesty International, the International Rescue Committee, and the Bainbridge Public Library.

A celebration of Kim will be held on Saturday, November 26, 2011, at 1:00 p.m. at The Church of Jesus Christ of Latter-day Saints on Bainbridge Island.

Acknowledgments

There is nothing in my life that I've done by myself. I have had a symphony of support surrounding me, including loving friends and family who have given me gifts from the heart.

Here are just a few of them, with a request for forgiveness to those who I've inadvertently left out:

Our community here at Winslow Cohousing. From the first moments through to the last, the support and attention have been extraordinary and critical. I am still comforted by the afghan knitted by many hands, by the sweet memories of the voices serenading us through the holidays at the rehab facility, by the seeming ease of day-to-day help for just about anything we needed.

Family who visited often. Sister **Susie** and bro-in-law **Kevin O'Brien** and nieces **Heather** and **Kate**; my nonagenarian relatives **Al and Sue Batzdorff**, who drove up from Santa Rosa more than a few times; Kim's daughter **Megan** and her mother **Judy Bush**, with first one, then two kids (Henry and Kimmy) in tow.

Henry was not yet three when Kim had his stroke. He showed up at the hospital after traveling across the country, bravely holding tight to a stuffed zebra and said, "I loved it up," and then handed it to his grandfather with a serious, sweet grace. There wasn't a night that that zebra wasn't in Kim's arms when he fell asleep. Henry has Kim's beautiful wide-open face that exudes kindness and curiosity. And **Kimmy**, although born just months before Kim passed, has somehow inherited Kim's playful mischievousness. (From where did he learn to put everything on his head?!)

Healers from many persuasions. **Alicia Valencia**, our young and vibrant caregiver who came every week for years, so important for both of us; **Julie Rosenblatt**, intuitive chiropractor who showed up at our home weekly without promise of reimbursement; **Elizabeth Turner**, who connected with Kim's psyche on a deep level; **Keith Heinzelman**, physical therapist extraordinaire, who made the impossible happen and nurtured a dynamic relationship where Kim wanted every day to be PT Day; **Susan Scott**, our therapist for years and my invaluable witness during this time; **Rodney Smith**, our guiding Buddhist teacher, for his continued teachings and care.

How grateful we are to have such a responsive **Emergency Medical System** (the paramedics got to know us well!) and **Harborview**, the best trauma hospital in the NW. **Dr. Khot** was the best neurologist one could hope for: patient, caring, attentive, and thorough.

Friends far and wide. Folks would stop by our room at the rehab facility just to see the solid wall of cards and well wishes, each one a reminder of the hearts that held us in their embrace. We received countless comments on our CarePages blog. And our little home had a revolving door of visitors.

A few folks stand out: **Nancy Pedersen**, my friend and a hospice nurse, the first to come to the hospital; **Tejavani and Archie McMillan**, who dropped everything and drove from Montana to offer friendship and rehab experience; **Linnaea Arnett**, who, at age eleven, had the courage to play "Ave Maria" on her violin for Kim while in the ICU; **Sharon Negri**, who slept alongside me on the hospital floor; **Rick Barrenger**, who turned our new place into an accessible home, recognizing that I had little brain to make decisions; **Sharon and Mark DuBois** for helping to ready our new place into the wee hours the night before I brought Kim home; **Chuck Beek**, who loves to shop and found the perfect recliner and van; the **Tuesday Night Sangha**, meditating with us for years; **Andy and Susan Griffiths** whose gift of a Bose system brought the world to us; **John Munson** for his reading to Kim every Wednesday; young **Travis McCoy**, who would come and delight us with his version of Scrabble; **Sarah Favret**, who showed up singing; **Jon Garfunkel** for bringing oysters and thought-provoking dialogue; **Michael and Alexa Rosenthal** for gifting me a year membership at their gym so I could keep my body strong enough to push Kim in his wheelchair ("Kim's Gym" we called it); **Cassie and Jim Gleckler**, ever-ready nurse consultants; **Cassie and Jim** along with **David Hager**, **Emily Groff**, and **Ranger and the Re-Arrangers** for gifting us with benefit concerts.

Also, **David and Judith Weinstock, Vicki Schoettle, Evy Marx**, and **Tony Abbondandolo** for generosity that helped make memories happen; **Linda Poh** for calmly walking me through legalities; **John Kenning** for seeing what Kim could do and helping him build a drum so that Kim could make audible his heartbeat; **Nellie Baker** and **Gordon Parke**, former heads of school at West Sound Academy, who believed in Kim and gave him opportunities to teach; **WSA's exceptional students** who came weekly to have meaningful discussions with Kim that fed his soul; **Kees**, the shipwright at the NW Maritime Heritage Center, for giving Kim's beloved peapod a home; **Barbara Saur** for accompanying us on our last great adventure to the high country; **Mary O'Hern** for staying connected from afar with her spiritual perspective and immense heart; **Joe Arnett**, who somehow thought of Bainbridge Island as "on the way home" from wherever he was, bringing a decades-long friendship of stories and song; to **Heather Geiser** for visioning a book hidden in my blog many years ago and presenting me with a hard copy; to **Mi Ae Lipe** for her careful attention to detail and invaluable guidance in creating a book; and to **Linn DeNesti**, former teacher and colleague of Kim's, for her patience, love, and extraordinary artistic eye.

And finally, to you, my beloved **Kim**. This bold, beautiful, brilliant, ever-playful and irreverent man. You lived your life richly and hungrily, inspiring me evermore. And your death broke open my heart so wide that I can love the world and not be afraid.

With bows and bouquets to all. ~ Judy

Reading Group Questions

1. How does your life experience intersect with Judy and Kim's story? What experiences, thoughts, or feelings resonate most with your own?

2. What strengths or qualities helped Judy manage four-plus years of caring for her husband? If you have been a caregiver or imagine being one, what strengths could you draw upon? What strengths would you like to develop?

3. Ever independent, Kim wanted acknowledgment that he was a "care receiver." What did it take for him to accept being cared for? What would be hard for you (if anything) to accept care?

4. How did Kim and Judy respond to the ever-changing landscape of their lives? How do you respond to change, especially when you do not choose it?

5. What care options did Judy and Kim have? What are the possibilities for long-term care in your area for someone who is disabled?

6. What does the word "summoned" in this book's title mean to you? To what life experiences or events have you been summoned?

7. Kim's stroke happened on a beautiful first day of fall while they were hiking. How do we live, knowing that change can happen at any time? Where does courage enter? Fear? Faith? Love? Humor?

8. Kim was always a risk-taker. How did that quality enrich his life? How did it make life more difficult? How did Judy and Kim balance safety versus freedom to live as fully as they could? Where are you on the continuum of risk—or safety?

9. Kim was a lifelong learner and global citizen. How did these approaches to life carry him through his poststroke years? What interests do you have that might help you move through times when you are less able?

10. Although Judy remained positive, she spoke of times where she "hit a wall" and she could not see a way to keep going. How do you move through setbacks?

11. Relationships of many kinds were invaluable to Kim and Judy's journey. What circles of support do you have to help sustain you in difficult times?

12. What part did gratitude play in Judy's ability to cope? How does gratitude show up in your life?

13. Reread the chapter titles. What do they tell you about the values in Kim and Judy's life? What values shape your life? How can your values help you live more fully each day, knowing that the unexpected is part of our life journey?

www.ingramcontent.com/pod-product-compliance
Lightning Source LLC
Chambersburg PA
CBHW051149290426
44108CB00019B/2665